Dante's
Divine
Comedy

Dante's *Divine Comedy*

A Biography

Joseph Luzzi

PRINCETON UNIVERSITY PRESS

PRINCETON & OXFORD

Published by Princeton University Press
41 William Street, Princeton, New Jersey 08540
99 Banbury Road, Oxford OX2 6JX

press.princeton.edu

Library of Congress Cataloging-in-Publication Data

Names: Luzzi, Joseph, author.
Title: Dante's Divine comedy : a biography / Joseph Luzzi.
Description: Princeton : Princeton University Press, 2024. |
    Includes bibliographical references and index.
Identifiers: LCCN 2024003730 (print) | LCCN 2024003731 (ebook) |
    ISBN 9780691156774 (hardback) | ISBN 9780691255644 (ebook)
Subjects: LCSH: Dante Alighieri, 1265–1321. Divina commedia. |
    Dante Alighieri, 1265–1321—Religion. | Dante Alighieri, 1265–1321—
    Appreciation. | LCGFT: Literary criticism.
Classification: LCC PQ4390 .L88 2024 (print) | LCC PQ4390 (ebook) |
    DDC 851/.1—dc23/eng/20240202
LC record available at https://lccn.loc.gov/2024003730
LC ebook record available at https://lccn.loc.gov/2024003731

British Library Cataloging-in-Publication Data is available

Editorial: Fred Appel and James Collier
Production Editorial: Karen Carter
Text and Jacket / Cover Design: Wanda España
Production: Erin Suydam
Publicity: Charlotte Coyne and Alyssa Sanford

Jacket/Cover Image: *The Barque of Dante*, Eugène Delacroix, 1822,
oil on canvas

This book has been composed in Arno Pro and Scrivano

Printed in the United States of America

10 9 8 7 6 5 4 3 2 1

For my brother and sisters,
Angelo, Margaret, Mary, Rose, and Tina
O sanguis meus

A ciascun'alma presa e gentil core
nel cui cospetto ven lo dir presente . . .
To every captive soul and gentle heart,
I now address these words of mine to you . . .

—DANTE, FIRST LINES OF POETRY, 1283

. . . l'amor che move il sole e l'altre stelle.
. . . the love that moves the sun and other stars.

—DANTE, LAST LINE OF POETRY, C. 1321

Contents

Dante's *Divine Comedy*

Introduction

NOT LONG before his death in 1321 at age fifty-six, a usually tough-minded poet let down his guard and admitted to his trials:

> If it should happen . . . If this sacred poem—
> this work so shared by heaven and by earth
> that it has made me lean through these long years—
> can ever overcome the cruelty
> that bars me from the fair [sheepfold] where I slept,
> a lamb opposed to wolves that war on it . . .

> *Se mai continga che 'l poema sacro*
> *al quale ha posto mano e cielo e terra,*
> *sì che m'ha fatto per molti anni macro,*
> *vinca la crudeltà che fuor mi serra*
> *del bello ovile ov' io dormi' agnello,*
> *nimico ai lupi che li danno guerra . . . (Par. 25.1–6)*[1]

It never would happen. Florence, the poet's "fair sheepfold," refused to recall him from exile, and he never realized his dream of being crowned poet laureate in his beloved Baptistery of San Giovanni, the holy site where he and all Florentine citizens were christened. This poet, of course, was Dante, a name so resounding that the above story is familiar to countless readers throughout the world.

Dante's melancholic avowal in *Paradiso* 25 of taking on a project as demanding as the work he called his *Comedìa*—the adjective "Divina" was only added to the title centuries later in 1555 by an enterprising Venetian printer—distills the essence of his complicated personality.[2] His relationship with Florence wavered between primal love and ferocious hatred, and he could never overcome the feeling of defeat and heartache brought on by his exile in 1302. He was confident of his own abilities to the point of occasional arrogance and braggadocio: in Limbo, this still-unproven poet has the chutzpah to list himself as the "sesto tra cotanto senno," "sixth among such intellects" (*Inf.* 4.102), a group of luminaries that includes Homer, Virgil, and Ovid. Dante believed he was on a mission from God: he called his work a "sacred poem" (*poema sacro*) and rightly anticipated that it would be the first epic to fuse secular and spiritual life into a seamless whole.

The confession scene in *Paradiso* 25 does more than take us inside Dante's obsessions and motivations: it also reveals that for the author of the *Commedia*, a 14,233-line work on the state of the soul after death written between about 1306 and 1321, the words *poetry* and *persona* were inseparable.[3] Almost every verse of consequence that Dante authored in his life, from his adolescent poems about his muse Beatrice that would be anthologized in the *Vita nuova* (New life, c. 1292–95) to the concluding passages in *Paradiso* on the poet's three mediated visions of his Christian God (including his view of Christ as "nostra effige," "our image," in the Holy Trinity, *Par.* 33.131),[4] centered in one way or another on Dante's own life experiences.[5] He was not an "autobiographer" in our modern sense of the word. The interiority and self-analysis implied by that term, which did not appear in English until 1797, would have been wholly out of place in Dante's deeply religious world. As he stated in his philosophical treatise *Il convivio* (The banquet, c. 1304–7) and implied in the *Commedia*, an author should write about one's name only out of necessity: to clear oneself from injustice, as Boethius had done in *De consolatione philosophiae* (The consolation of philosophy, c. 524), or to establish a model for Christians to follow, in the manner of Augustine in his groundbreaking *Confessiones* (Confessions, 397–400).[6] Dante believed he was checking both of those boxes. To his dying breath, he considered the ban of exile levied against him unjust, and throughout his epic poem he wrote with the conviction of a religious prophet nominated— albeit *self*-nominated—to help humanity save their Christian souls.

The tendency, historically, has been for nonspecialist readers to focus more on Dante's damned than his blessed, a bias expressed memorably by Victor Hugo, who claimed, "[Dante] was somewhat at home in hell, but he is no longer so in heaven. He cannot recognize himself in angels. The human eye is perhaps not made for so much sun; and when the poem draws happiness, it becomes tedious."[7] There have been notable dissents to Hugo's opinion: as we will see, T. S. Eliot believed that the poetry of *Paradiso* was the greatest ever written, and Matthew Arnold located a "perfect" line of verse in the same canticle.[8] But many today are likely to be sympathetic with Hugo as they take on the most explicitly religious—and doctrinal—part of Dante's poem, which Robert Hollander describes as the "most challenging" in all Dante, adding, "One finds few who will claim (or admit) that [*Paradiso*] is their favorite *cantica*."[9] Dante's spirituality has elicited conflicting reactions for centuries: what inspires one reader in his religious vision is just as likely to cause confusion or raise hackles in another. It can be difficult, at a distance of seven hundred years and with a writer as celebrated as Dante, to remember that his life was one of dramatic bets. An intensely experimental writer, he took the enormous risk of writing his epic poem in a regional dialect, Tuscan, instead of the scholarly language of choice, Latin, because he was committed to forging a new literary tradition rooted in his native cultural soil. And he multiplied that risk by writing about *himself*, a struggling Florentine exile, when his epic predecessors had sung of such lofty themes as the Trojan War, the homecoming of Odysseus, and the founding of Rome. It is no wonder that his religious vision would turn out to be just as idiosyncratic and divisive as the poetic project that inspired it.

Yet it was precisely Dante's willingness to roll the literary dice, to endure peril and embrace uncertainty, that makes what he achieved so remarkable—and his religious vision so original. Using the same brio with which he translated his personal story into an epic poem, Dante rankled the conventionally religious with his extraordinary claim of having been given the beatific vision while still in the flesh. More than this, he granted himself this sublime privilege because of the alleged intercession of the muse he worshiped from afar, Beatrice, whom he transformed into an intimate associate of the exalted Virgin Mary as well as his patron saint, Saint Lucy of Syracuse, a martyr and champion of the blind and those who struggle with their eyesight (as Dante himself did). According to Joan M. Ferrante, Dante's cult of Beatrice also shaped his understanding of the relation between religion and gender:

> It is a commonplace of Dante criticism that the poet's love for Beatrice leads him to God, literally within the poem and figuratively within his life. But it does a good deal more than that. It also leads him to see a feminine side in God, in the human race, and in himself.[10]

Adding fuel to the polemical fires surrounding his religious views, Dante also took every chance he could to excoriate the leaders of his church, lambasting one pope after another, from the "neutral" Celestine V in *Inferno* 3 to his perennial bête noire, Boniface VIII, in the canto of the Simonists, *Inferno* 19.[11] All told, no fewer than five popes are individually targeted for Dante's hell. Not one to court the opinion of the crowd, Dante went straight to the top for affirmation of his attack on Church corruption: in *Paradiso* 27, Saint Peter, Christ's apostle and founder of the Catholic Church, skewers Boniface VIII with these words:

> "He who on earth usurps my place, my place,
> my place that in the sight of God's own Son
> is vacant now, has made my burial ground
> a sewer of blood, a sewer of stench, so that
> the perverse one who fell from Heaven, here
> above, can find contentment there below."

> *"Quelli ch'usurpa in terra il luogo mio,*
> *il luogo mio, il luogo mio, che vaca*
> *ne la presenza del Figliuol di Dio,*
> *fatt' ha del cimitero mio cloaca*
> *del sangue e de la puzza; onde 'l perverso*
> *che cadde di qua sù, là giù si placa."* (22–27)

If ever there were an indicator of Dante's own anger toward the Christian hierarchy, it was this repetition of "my place" (*luogo mio*) emerging in three surging beats from the mouth of Saint Peter.

The ongoing tension between Dante's personal story and the Christian nature of his poem, the source of his religious vision's originality as well as its divisiveness, has driven the reception history of the *Commedia*. In an influential meditation from 1942, the scholar and seminarian Bruno Nardi asked simply but incisively, "Was Dante really a prophet?"[12] In Nardi's view, the answer was an emphatic *yes*: "Now it seems to me that if we think with an unprejudiced mind of what the great inspired men and the seers of the Old Testament represented in the historical framework of the religion of Israel, Dante really continued its tradition and language, so as to deserve being considered a prophet as they were."[13] Nardi qualified his assertion, adding that many of Dante's political predictions were inaccurate, which might tempt one to call him a "false" prophet. But in reality, he continued, like all "true" and "great" prophets, Dante managed to lift his poetry "beyond the events that were occurring beneath his eyes and show an eternal ideal of justice as the criterion for measuring the moral stature of men and the value of their actions. . . . The man who is used to giving ear to the low voices rising from the nether depth of consciousness and to fixing his gaze within the light shining in the innermost recesses of the soul is not dismayed if the external world shatters around him because he has found what is sufficient to him and cannot be taken from him: God."[14]

Nardi's rousing insight was a major moment in the religious afterlife of Dante's epic not only because of what he said but also for the responses that he would elicit. Teodolinda Barolini remarked that Nardi's words have led readers to the fundamental question of Dante's poem: "How are we to respond to the poet's insistence that he is telling us the truth?"[15] Invoking Charles Singleton's influential claim that "the fiction of the *Divine Comedy* is that it is not a fiction,"[16] Barolini notes how "Singleton's heirs dig ever more deeply into the cultural and theological humus from which the *Commedia* grows [and] make the poet appear more and more a theologian, unleashing a backlash from those who would have us remember that he is a poet."[17] Looking to move past this critical impasse, Barolini proposes that "we read the *Commedia* less theologically and more practically," so that we can paradoxically "detheologize our reading if we are to understand what makes the theology stick."[18]

This dialogue between the religious and poetic strands in the *Commedia* has defined its centuries-long "biography" or afterlife among readers. On the one hand, as Peter Hawkins writes, "That Dante's *Commedia* is a religious poem, even a 'divine' one, seems to go without saying. Indeed, for the Christian West, it has come to set the gold standard for what such a work should be."[19] Yet, Hawkins counters, resistance to Dante's religious message has been immediate and perennial: as early as 1327, the Dominican friar Guido Vernani dubbed Dante the "Devil's vessel," and in 1335, the Dominican superiors declared the *Commedia* off-limits to both impressionable novices and seasoned members of the order.[20] While Dante has gone on to become in our own times what Hawkins calls "court poet" of the Vatican, the idiosyncratic nature of his religious vision has continued to inspire as well as rankle readers.[21] Harold Bloom spoke of Dante as "a ruthless visionary, passionately ambitious and desperately willful, whose poem triumphantly expresses his own unique personality."[22] Similarly, for James Miller, Dante negotiated the "contested border between Literature and Belief" and succeeded in making "a triumphantly orthodox poem out of his immediately transgressive experiences."[23]

In the aggregate, responses to the *Commedia* reveal how the poem thrives on its productive tensions: it promotes Virgil to the role of guide while denigrating his pagan age as one of "false and lying gods" ("dèi falsi e bugiardi," *Inf.* 1.72); it excoriates individual popes while upholding the sanctity of the papacy itself; and it promotes the virtues of humility and modesty while proclaiming Dante's own poetic superiority. Similarly, the intense religiosity of the poem has always been shadowed by its earthly concerns, as we see in these words from William Franke:

> Dante stands in certain outstanding respects as the premier secularizing thinker and writer of the modern age. The concrete world of history and human individuality emerges from his work with unprecedented force and clarity. It emerges, moreover, as a revelation of an ultimate, eschatological reality of the other world translated into a symbolic language of the phenomena of this world realistically perceived and represented.[24]

The "secular" Dante is most famously associated with the German philologist Erich Auerbach and his landmark study *Dante als Dichter der irdischen Welt* (Dante as poet of the secular world, 1929). Emphasizing the link between Dante's religious vision and personal experience, Auerbach notes that the two were ultimately symbiotic: "The content of the *Comedy* is a vision; but what is beheld in the vision is the truth as concrete reality, and hence it is both real and rational."[25]

Auerbach's "realist" Dante has an illustrious genealogy, including the legendary critic Francesco De Sanctis, whose *Storia della letteratura italiana* (History of Italian literature, 1871–72) helped create a sense of common cultural identity in the newly formed Italian nation. De Sanctis began writing on *Inferno* 5 as early as 1854, and his realist interpretation of Dante culminated in his description of Francesca da Rimini, the star-crossed lover from the Circle of the Lustful in *Inferno* 5: "Francesca, as Dante conceived her, is more alive and real than she could ever be as presented by history."[26] De Sanctis claimed that the flesh-and-blood Francesca piqued the reader's interest in a way that Dante's more generic and abstract muse Beatrice never could: "In this genial creation [Francesca] are contained the seeds of the finest creations of modern poetry, having at their center woman as released from metaphysics and mysticism and understood as a living person."[27] De Sanctis glossed over the harsh nature of Francesca's sin and damnation; what interested him was the vividness of her character and the force of her literary portrait. His sympathy for her is palpable throughout the essay—one feels as though, like Dante the protagonist, he was seduced by her winning words and gracious manners, leaving him with little patience for the stark Christian judgment that situates her in hell.

Not surprisingly, Dante's deeply personal approach to poetry and faith led him to an obsession over how his work would be read. The *Commedia* contains some twenty addresses to the reader, establishing an intimacy with his audience that was unprecedented.[28] If ever there were an epic poem with its own instructions for use, it was Dante's, with exhortations like "O you possessed of sturdy intellects, / observe the teaching that is hidden here / beneath the veil of verses so obscure" (*O voi ch'avete li 'ntelletti sani, / mirate la dottrina che s'asconde / sotto 'l velame de li versi strani, Inf.* 9.61–63).[29] Scholars continue to debate whether or not Dante wrote the celebrated and controversial "Letter to Cangrande," with its injunction that Dante's poetry be read on four levels, the literal, moral, allegorical, and anagogical or spiritual.[30] Though the question of authorship remains open, I agree with scholars who believe that what matters is that Dante *could have* written the "Letter to Cangrande": it squares with Dante's actual literary practice and the enormous semantic pressure he puts on the lines of his poem and their polyvalent meanings.

The celebrated opening of the *Commedia*—"When I had journeyed half of our life's way / I found myself within a shadowed forest" (*Nel mezzo del cammin di nostra vita / mi ritrovai per una selva oscura, Inf.* 1.1–2)—illustrates the possibilities of interpretation inherent in Dante's writing. The lines are *literal* in that Dante, at the fictional date of the poem, 1300, is thirty-five years old, half of the biblical life as established in the Book of Isaiah 38:10. The moral, allegorical, and anagogical levels follow suit: Dante goes to hell, following in the footsteps of Jesus as narrated in Ephesians 4:9. And the supremely allegorical *selva oscura*, shadowed forest or dark wood, is hardly an actual woodland setting in Dante's Florence: it is rather the space of Christian error and sin, a hallowed trope in religious literature.[31]

The vertiginous amount of interpretation spun off by Dante's lines has made him one of the most commented-upon authors in history. From 1950 and to 1970 alone, nearly ten thousand articles were written on his work, and a recent guide from the Modern Language Association of America offers pedagogical advice for learning about Dante through music, gender, and different artistic media, among many other topics, and in a manual geared for audiences including high school seniors and incarcerated prisoners.[32] Physical copies of the responses to Dante's work over the arc of seven centuries would fill a good-sized library. Yet the *Commedia* is hardly the mere province of scholars: numerous contemporary books and films employ imagery from Dante's afterlife, more than one hot sauce has the word *Inferno* emblazoned on it, and everything from the local motor vehicles outpost and megastore shopping aisles to online dating and passenger-jet seating has been compared to Dante's circles of hell. His ubiquity extends from the lowbrow and middlebrow to the loftiest altitudes of cultural expression. There is an *Inferno* video game with an improbably muscle-bound Dante who rescues his beloved Beatrice after ceaseless mortal combat. His name appears on olive oils, wines, even a toilet paper ad. On the other end of the spectrum, one of the oldest cultural societies in the United States, the Dante Society of America, was founded in 1881 by such leading cultural figures as Henry Wadsworth Longfellow, Charles Eliot Norton, and James Russell Lowell, and early participants included Henry David Thoreau and Ralph Waldo Emerson, a translator of Dante's *Vita nuova*. T. S. Eliot, in typically oracular assessment, was perhaps not exaggerating when he said, "Dante and Shakespeare divide the modern world between them, there is no third."[33]

One thing becomes clear to anyone who hopes to write a biography of Dante's magnum opus, *The Divine Comedy*, and its secular and spiritual impact: a chronological or geographical survey is out of the question, unless one plans to spend a lifetime compiling the oceanic amount of material and trying to convince one's editor to publish a work whose pages would perforce run into the tens if not hundreds of thousands. The recent decades in particular have seen a salubrious expansion of studies on Dante's far-reaching influence outside of the traditional Anglo-European context and into such areas as his presence among historically marginalized writers and the *Commedia*'s impact in popular media forms outside of the literary and visual arts.[34] In full awareness of the necessarily selective and personal approach of my own attempt to account for Dante's afterlife—and of course cognizant that other authors tasked with this responsibility would have produced studies of a very different kind—I have chosen to remain largely within the confines of my own scholarly expertise in the history of Western literature and feature those paradigmatic moments in Dante's reception that coalesce into a narrative whose individual parts are often in dialogue with one another. In so doing, I have tried to follow Dante's own intensely synthetic habits of mind and approach the afterlife of the *Commedia* as systematically as possible. As Jorge Luis Borges once said, it takes a modern novel hundreds of pages to lay bare the essence of a character, whereas for Dante a few dozen verses will do.[35] My hope is that this same drive for concision and synthesis can work for exploring his epic's afterlife.

Distilling the reception of the *Commedia* to its essence requires a form of rhetorical mapping that would have come natural to Dante, one of the most incisive interpreters of linguistic and literary form ever. As vast as the reception of Dante's epic has been, certain topoi or recurring elements emerge. Any invocation of the term *topos*,[36] which refers to a traditional or conventional literary or rhetorical theme or topic, recalls the practice developed by Ernst Robert Curtius in his landmark study *Europäische Literatur und lateinisches Mittelalter* (European literature and the Latin Middle Ages, 1948).[37] Curtius mapped out a system of the Latin works produced in the medieval period by discovering what literary motifs and forms were constantly repeated and reflective of patterns.[38] These tropes enabled him to construct a rhetorical "forest" from the individual "trees" of Latin medieval texts, a methodology that also works well for charting the afterlife of the *Commedia*.

My mention of literary trees and forests might suggest that I am invoking a practice similar to the provocative model developed by Franco Moretti and his notion of "distant reading," which takes a bird's-eye view of literature and uses statistics, graphs, and other indicators of literary production to create literary histories that dispense with the traditional practices of close reading.[39] I am emphatically not following Moretti, as the following pages will show. The Dantesque topoi that emerge from the centuries-long afterlife of his *Commedia* are all ones that can be accessed only by the kind of careful interpretation of individual textual details that Moretti's model eschews. As we will see, these topoi include Dante as champion of the vernacular in early Italian literature, Dante as religious heretic during the Inquisition, Dante as literary hero for the Romantics, Dante as formal innovator for the Modernists, and Dante as religious visionary for modern-day popes, to name only some of his more prominent manifestations and to give a sense of their variety and expansiveness. In adducing this list, I make no pretense of offering a comprehensive or "quantitative" understanding of how and why the *Commedia* has been read since its appearance in the early 1300s. Instead, my focus will be on what seem to be the most consequential and representative elements of that literary afterlife, as represented by topoi whose looming presence and influence I believe justify their selection.

In seeking to choose the topoi that define the afterlife of Dante's *Commedia* and constitute its biography, Dante himself is once again our guide. By personalizing his epic to an unprecedented degree, and by interlacing instructions on how to read his poem within its dense fabric of verses and manifold references to everything from history and politics to theology and poetics among much else, Dante did more than shape the influence of his work: he helped create it. In reading responses to the *Commedia* as varied as Franco Sacchetti's stories about the hotheaded character Dante in his *Il trecentonovelle* (Three hundred tales, 1399) and Sandow Birk's edgy urban illustrations of *Inferno* (2003),[40] one can almost feel Dante's ghost smiling knowingly, unsurprised at the protean forms his work has inspired. Ultimately, the plurality of these responses validates Dante's decision to write a poem so challengingly "encyclopedic," to invoke Giuseppe Mazzotta's term, that it has engendered a corresponding interpretive and creative surplus.[41]

An episode from early in the *Commedia* suggests Dante's uncanny ability to anticipate and even encourage his own reception history. Around 1295, years before beginning his epic *Commedia*, Dante dedicated the *Vita nuova* to the man he called his "best friend" (*primo amico*), the supremely talented Guido Cavalcanti, a leader of the Sweet New Style, the poetic movement that nurtured the young Dante's writing and fused lyrical refinement and natural philosophy in writing about "angel women" (*donne angelicate*) like Beatrice. Astonishingly, just several years later in 1300 and in his capacity as one of Florence's six priors, the highest elected official in the city, Dante signed an edict banishing the radical Cavalcanti from the city. Cavalcanti died later that year, in August 1300, from malaria contracted abroad. Dante himself was exiled in 1302; when he began the *Commedia* around 1306, he handled his role in his best friend's demise with breathtaking defensiveness. The fictional date of *The Divine Comedy* is April 1300, so Guido still lives. In *Inferno* 10, where the sin of heresy is punished—"all those who say the soul dies with the body" (*che l'anima col corpo morta fanno*, 15)—Dante encounters Guido's Epicurean father, Cavalcante de' Cavalcanti, who burns for this same heretical philosophy associated with his son. "If it is your high intellect / that lets you journey here, through this blind prison [hell], / where is my son? Why is he not with you?," Guido's father asks (*Inf.* 10.58–60).[42] Your son, Dante tells him, perhaps "did disdain" (*ebbe a disdegno*) Dante's guide through hell (Virgil, Beatrice, or God Himself; the pronoun referent "*cui*" in *Inf.* 10.63, "one" or "whom," is left unclear). Guido's father hears *ebbe a disdegno*, the absolute past (*passato remoto*) form "did disdain," and assumes that his son, like the verb, is in the past tense. He asks, "The sweet light does not strike against [Guido's] eyes?" (*non fiere li occhi suoi lo dolce lumen?*, *Inf.* 10.69). Dante hesitates in replying. This guilty heartbeat of a pause signals to Cavalcante de' Cavalcanti that his son is dead, and so he falls into the broth of hell "and did not show himself again" (*e più non parve fora, Inf.* 10.72). Dante never referred, directly or indirectly, to his best friend's death again.

Seven centuries of scholarly inquiry have not yet revealed exactly to whom that mysterious pronoun *cui* refers. Many scholars have strong opinions as to the person in question, but ultimately only Dante himself knew.[43] The episode is just one of several in which it is impossible to know exactly what Dante means or refers to: Why does Ulysses in *Inferno* 26 forsake his long-lost Ithaca for "experience of the world"? Did Ugolino from *Inferno* 33 actually cannibalize his children? What does the Roman numeral "DXV" in *Purgatorio* 33 signify? The list goes on, leaving the reader to fill in some mighty blanks. Countless commentators have taken the Dantesque bait and done their best to answer on the poet's behalf. The result has been mountains of scholarship poking through clouds of speculation, in an atmosphere of heated debate that expands with each generation. The poet and Dante commentator extraordinaire Percy Bysshe Shelley described the situation best when he called great poetry like Dante's a "fountain forever overflowing with the waters of wisdom and delight; and after one person and one age has exhausted all its divine effluence which their peculiar relations enable them to share, another and yet another succeeds, and new relations are ever developed, the source of an unforeseen and an unconceived delight."[44] It's no wonder that the essay in which these words appear, "A Defence of Poetry" (1821), devotes large sections to Dante and his "inexhaustible fountain of purity of sentiment and language."

Shelley did more than articulate a general theory of how certain literary works remain evergreen by captivating readers separated from their moments of composition by huge swaths of time and space. He specifically invoked the rhetoric of invention and discovery that has helped generate many of the topoi associated with the afterlife of the *Commedia*:

> Dante was the first religious reformer, and Luther surpassed him rather in the rudeness and acrimony, than in the boldness of his censures of papal usurpation. Dante was the first awakener of entranced Europe; he created a language, in itself music and persuasion, out of a chaos of inharmonious barbarisms.

The passage reveals two elements central to the biography of Dante's epic: its impact as a religious work *and* as a poetic text. Indeed, Shelley's point on the latter is startlingly accurate, for his claim that Dante's language fused "music and persuasion" rhymes with Dante's own assertion in his groundbreaking treatise on the Romance languages, *De vulgari eloquentia* (On eloquence in the vernacular, c. 1302–5), which argues that "poetry is rhetoric [persuasion] set to music."[45] This language of firsts adduced by Shelley resurfaces repeatedly in the afterlife of Dante's work and has conditioned the topoi associated with his originality.

The dialogue between poetic originality and religious doctrine is present from the start of the *Commedia*. In *Inferno* 1, Dante meets his initial guide, Virgil, who has been sent by the Virgin Mary, after Beatrice's appeal to her, to aid the lost pilgrim. The proverbial fame of Virgil's Latin epic poem, the *Aeneid*, would seem to make Dante's choice logical enough. But readers often forget just how unusual, even scandalous, Dante's decision was to select a pagan and nonbeliever as his guide through the first leg of the Christian afterlife. Virgil's secular brilliance made him an apt commentator on the issues of sin and transgression, crime and punishment, in *Inferno*—but so would have countless other Christian exemplars of literary genius, including ones who themselves wrote spiritual autobiographies or conversion narratives like Dante's, especially Saint Augustine.[46] Yet Dante opts for Virgil primarily because he has a special affinity for his writing, which engendered the "long study and the intense love" (*lungo studio e 'l grande amore, Inf.* 1.83) that led him to the *Aeneid.* As the pilgrim continues his spiritual journey beyond hell and into purgatory, the scandal of Virgil's presence only intensifies: at least the Latin poet's brilliant understanding of human error and transgression qualified him to comment on the issues of *Inferno,* but in the Christian spaces of *Purgatorio* he is truly in terra incognita, as his bizarre colloquy with the gatekeeper Cato reveals. When Dante and Virgil arrive in the second canticle, Virgil asks his fellow Roman to give his charge special treatment as they wend their way up the mountain of purgation, promising to put in a good word with Cato's wife, Marcia, whose spirit resides below in Virgil's Limbo:

"Allow our journey through your seven realms.
I shall thank her for kindness you bestow—
if you would let your name be named below."

"*Lasciane andar per li tuoi sette regni;
grazie riporterò di te a lei,
se d' esser mentovato là giù degni.*" (*Purg.* 1.82–84)

The tactic is embarrassingly ineffective: the stern guardian Cato denies any interest in his unredeemed wife, reminding Virgil that after his Christian conversion he wishes to please an entirely different kind of woman, one on the other side of the "evil river" (*mal fiume,* 88) that now separates him, literally and figuratively, from Marcia:

"While I was there, within the other world,
Marcia so pleased my eyes," [Cato] then replied,
"each kindness she required, I satisfied.

Now that she dwells beyond the evil river,
she has no power to move me any longer,
such was the law decreed when I was freed.
But if a lady come from Heaven speeds
and helps you, as you say, there is no need
of flattery; it is enough, indeed,
to ask me for her sake."

"Marzïa piacque tanto a li occhi miei
mentre ch'i' fu' di là," diss' elli allora,
"che quante grazie volse da me, fei.
Or che di là dal mal fiume dimora,
più muover non mi può, per quella legge
che fatta fu quando me n'usci' fora.
Ma se donna del ciel ti muove e regge,
come tu di', non c'è mestier lusinghe:
bastisi ben che per lei mi richegge." (85–93)

Cato's rejection of Marcia in favor of Beatrice reveals a new
spiritual worldview that is forever closed to the pagan Virgil, the
once-redoubtable guide of hell who is increasingly ill at ease—
and short on valuable advice—the higher he and Dante climb
up Mount Purgatory.

Yet the intimacy between Dante and Virgil from *Inferno* 1
onward, up to Dante's tearful realization in *Purgatorio* 30 that
the Latin poet has left him, can make us forget that more than
a millennium separated the two. All that distance, religious,
chronological, and otherwise, collapses as Virgil is transformed,
right on the page before us, into Dante's beloved *duca* and *mae-*
stro, leader and teacher, even his "sweetest father" (*dolcissimo*
patre). Dante's Virgil, in the manner of all literary interpretations and transformations, is highly individual, even eccentric.
The Florentine poet was drawn to the Roman poet not just

because of his beautiful writing but also because he represented the sense of imperial mission Dante desperately craved for the Italian peninsula. Virgil was also the cultural embodiment of an epic style—and cultural prestige—that Dante wished to make his own. A similar mix of emotions and ambitions would motivate many readers and writers throughout history to choose Dante as their "guide" with a passion equal to the one that had drawn him to Virgil.

In embarking on the early chapters of the *Commedia*'s reception, we should remember the poet's opening words in the *Vita nuova*: "In my Book of Memory, in the early part where there is little to be read, there comes a chapter with the rubric: *Here begins the new life*" (*In quella parte del libro de la mia memoria dinanzi a la quale poco si potrebbe leggere, si trova una rubrica la quale dice:* Incipit vita nova).[47] It is no stretch to say that much of the *Commedia* that followed decades later would be a variation on these interlacing motifs of memory, spiritual rebirth, and the literary construction of the writer's life.[48] Dante goes on to write in the *Vita nuova*, "It is my intention to copy into this little book the words I find written under that chapter—if not all of them, at least the essence of their meaning" (*Sotto la quale rubrica io trovo scritte le parole le quali è mio intendimento d'assemplare in questo libello; e se non tutte, almeno la loro sentenzia*).[49] And so it must be with a life, a *vita*, of Dante's *Commedia*. The extensive quantity of the reception history makes writing all of the words written in response to Dante's work impossible; the best one can hope for, in the spirit of the *Vita nuova*, are representative chapters that capture the essence of Dante's meaning.

Chapter 1

Inventing "Italian" Literature

TOWARD THE MIDDLE of the *Vita nuova*—and soon before the dramatic premature death of Beatrice at age twenty-four that transforms the book's narrative and, with it, the author's life— Dante describes why he has chosen to personify Love, the ominous figure who appeared to him in a dream carrying the naked body of Beatrice in his arms while she devoured his burning heart before his dumbstruck eyes. "Formerly," he wrote, "there were no love poets writing in the vernacular, the only love poets were those writing in Latin . . . it was not vernacular poets but learned poets who wrote about love."[1] The clunky, repetitive, and overly explicit prose is typical of Dante's explanations for his poetic choices in the *Vita nuova*. And with good reason. Dante wished to be exceedingly clear to the point of pedantry because he had an important goal in mind. Basically, he sought to forge, ex nihilo, a literary tradition in an "Italian" tongue that did not yet exist, an ambition that would compel him to systematize his thoughts on the subject in *De vulgari eloquentia*.[2]

To understand the scale of Dante's dream of creating a local poetic language that shared the prestige and elegance of Latin, we need to dwell on the word *vernacular* for a moment. Dante's

Tuscan term for it, *volgare*, has a suggestive etymology, deriving
from the Latin *vulgus*, meaning "people, plebs, the masses."
More dramatically, the word derives from *vernaculus*, or "domestic, native," which originated with the Latin *verna*, a female
"home-born slave." That Dante's word *volgare* and its cognates
should have roots in disadvantage, bondage, and servitude is
fitting, for it reveals the ongoing literary battle that Dante fought
from the start of his career. He had that same overwhelming
sense of mission as a later writer, Germany's Goethe, who trav-
eled to Italy to immerse himself in classical forms and bring
back to his fragmented nation the refined and prestigious literary language that he believed it lacked, earning him the tag of
"belated Renaissancer."[3]

Dante was arguably that solo Renaissance for Italy. Jacob
Burckhardt described him as the one "who first thrust antiquity
into the foreground of national culture," a characterization that
squares with Dante's words in the *Vita nuova* on how vernacular
poets who write about love are following in the footsteps of
great ancient authors including Ovid, Horace, Lucan, and of
course his future guide, Virgil.[4] This infusion of the ancient into
the modern became a prime justification for the *Vita nuova*,
which aimed to show that a thirteenth-century Florentine poet
could write about a subject as storied as love with the same fi-
nesse and cultural imprimatur as the Latin authors Italians
claimed as their patrimony. Dante's embrace of antiquity was
both a self-justification and a warning: "let me add that just as
the Latin poets did not write in the way they did without a reason, so vernacular poets should not write in the same way without having a reason for writing as they do," he claimed, recalling
certain "clumsy" contemporaries guilty of not following this
precept.[5]

Such efforts on behalf of the literary vernacular connect to Dante's religious vision. With the same proselytizing spirit that compelled him to try to establish a literary tradition in the Tuscan, he pushed the limits of orthodoxy by raising himself, by his own literary fiat, to the status of prophet and religious authority, one allegedly anointed by heaven to spread the Christian word in the dialect of his hometown. The end result of this superhuman literary and religious ambition resulted in that rarest of things: a work, the *Commedia*, that was written in the vernacular but that was also epic in scope and bore testament to a private experience that proposed to encompass all of humanity's spiritual needs, distilled into a pervading tension between self, world, and afterlife that is evident from the first line of the poem to the last.[6]

The question must now be asked why Dante would go to such lengths, much farther than any of his fellow poets in the Sweet New Style, in defending the vernacular. It is no stretch to say that Dante's defense of the vernacular, from its seeds in the *Vita nuova* to its full theoretical blossoming in *De vulgari eloquentia*, was the aesthetic lodestar of his career, culminating in his fateful decision to write his masterpiece, the *Commedia*, in the Tuscan dialect. To write that epic in Latin would have made eminent sense from a practical point of view. Latin was, after all, the lingua franca of the international scholarly community. Thus, a Latin version of Dante's poem could have been read in all the major intellectual centers of Europe, from Paris and London and the Germanic lands in the north to points south in Spain and beyond. Deciding to write in Tuscan placed severe limitations on the poem's reception: it could only truly be understood in the immediate vicinity of Florence and neighboring areas, since even within Italy the differences in dialect were considerable and enduring. As late as the nineteenth century,

Milanese nobles traveling to Sicily were mistaken for Englishmen, so incomprehensible was their language to the locals.[7]

In *De vulgari eloquentia*, Dante developed his views on the necessity of the vernacular by describing how poets preserve what is lasting and lovely in everyday speech, preventing language from slipping into oblivion and mere instrumentality.[8] He chose to write his *Commedia* in Tuscan and not Latin because he knew that no mere scholarly or "dead" language could capture the intimate rhythms, cadences, and meanings of everyday speech and, by extension, the resonances and experiences of daily life. It is no wonder that a later author, James Joyce, would take Dante as a model in writing his own vernacular epic on the quotidian, *Ulysses* (1922), a work laced with puns, jokes, and salty turns of phrase in the dialect. Only the vernacular could serve such simultaneously ambitious yet homespun epic functions for both the Florentine poet and Irish novelist.

The *Commedia* abounds with gestures toward the fleeting, mortal, and timebound nature of human language and its poetic capabilities. In *Purgatorio* 11, Dante meets the shade of the great manuscript illuminator, Oderisi da Gubbio, who gives him an impromptu lesson on the ephemeral nature of artistic fame:

> "In painting Cimabue thought he held
> the field, and now it's Giotto they acclaim—
> the former only keeps a shadowed fame.
> So did one Guido, from the other, wrest
> the glory of our tongue—and he perhaps
> is born who will chase both out of the nest."

> *"Credette Cimabue ne la pittura*
> *tener lo campo, e ora ha Giotto il grido,*
> *sì che la fama di colui è scura:*

così ha tolto l'uno a l'altro Guido
la gloria de la lingua; e forse è nato
chi l'uno e l'altro caccerà del nido." (94–99)

Several cantos later, in *Purgatorio* 26, Dante will meet one of the two Guidos, Guido Guinizelli, a Bolognese founder of the Sweet New Style who appears among those who purge what Dante calls "hermaphrodite" desire, excessive heterosexual lust. Overwhelmed with devotion at his encounter with his literary forebear, Dante writes:

And I to him: "It's your sweet lines that, for
as long as modern usage lasts, will still
make dear their very inks."

E io a lui: "Li dolci detti vostri,
che, quanto durerà l'uso moderno,
faranno cari ancora i loro incostri." (112–14)

The lines make astonishing use of the word *modern* (*moderno* in Dante's original), signaling that it is a relative rather than an absolute term meant to invoke the new and contemporary and indicating that as gorgeously as a poet like Guinizelli or anyone for that matter writes, eventually their "dear ink" will dry and new poets, with new poetic forms, will supplant them. Not surprisingly, this is the very notion that Dante picks up a canticle later, in *Paradiso* 26, where the biblical Adam has the final word on the matter of linguistic temporality:

"The tongue I spoke was all extinct before
the men of Nimrod set their minds upon
the unaccomplishable task; for never
has anything produced by human reason
been everlasting—following the heavens,

men seek the new, they shift their predilections.
That man should speak at all is nature's act,
but how you speak—in this tongue or in that—
she leaves to you and to your preference."

"La lingua ch'io parlai fu tutta spenta
innanzi che a l'ovra inconsummabile
fosse la gente di Nembròt attenta:
ché nullo effetto mai razïonabile,
per lo piacere uman che rinovella
seguendo il cielo, sempre fu durabile.
Opera naturale è ch'uom favella;
ma così o così, natura lascia
poi fare a voi secondo che v'abbella." (124–32)

The message is clear: the linguistic usage of mortals, Adam
notes—echoing Horace—is like a "leaf on a branch": one generation speaks as it will, to be succeeded by another, which in
turn uses new words in new ways, all part of "nature's act."[9] The
vernacular is the child of time, which in Dante's poetic theory
becomes the ultimate arbiter of all literary and by extension
cultural endeavors. This radical notion would drive the first incarnation of Dante's afterlife.

Typically for the *Commedia*, religious concerns joined hands
with aesthetic ones in inspiring Dante's embrace of what many
considered the uncouth vernacular. As Erich Auerbach notes in
Literary Language and Its Public in Late Latin Antiquity and in the
Middle Ages (1958), Dante was among the Christian writers who
understood that "the 'lowliness' of the Biblical style" could
possess a "profound sublimity" that had previously only been
associated with the elite literary discourse of Latin.[10] Dante not
only infused his writing with the accessible vernacular typical of
the *sermo umilis*, the "humble speech" that enabled religious in-

stitutions to disseminate the wisdom of the Gospel to the masses, but he also correctly intuited that a growing readership outside of Church walls would actively consume this literary idiom. Auerbach describes how Dante "created a public for himself and for his successor as well. . . . When Dante wrote—shortly after 1300—the ability to read and write and the need for literary entertainment seem . . . to have attained roughly the same level as in Roman Italy just before the classical period."[11] Emphasizing the role of the biblically infused vernacular in Dante's rise to popularity, Auerbach concludes that Dante's "manner of handling language and of dealing with things in language, exerted an influence, first in Italy and gradually, through the Italian literature of the fourteenth century, elsewhere as well."[12]

The immediate reception history of the *Commedia* confirms Auerbach's claim that Dante was able to invent a new reading public. Manuscript versions of his epic began to circulate in earnest while the poet was still alive. Indeed, Dante would achieve that most coveted of literary feats: he garnered both the critical acclaim of leading contemporaries who proclaimed his genius and a popular appeal that extended beyond the narrow confines of the scholarly world and into the growing middle class of clerks, scribes, book collectors, and other literary enthusiasts who were establishing the cultural rites and institutions that would give rise to Renaissance humanism. By the end of the 1300s, about eight hundred manuscripts of the *Commedia* were in circulation. Legends about Dante's literary reach even began to form: one, eventually dismissed as apocryphal, alleged that a particularly industrious scribe named Francesco di ser Nardo da Barberino produced a hundred copies of the *Commedia* in order to pad his daughters' dowries with their proceeds.[13] The extravagance of this legend attests to the mix of fact and hearsay that attended the posthumous ascent of Dante's reputation.

A vigorous commentary tradition on Dante's epic poem also sprang up immediately after the poet's death, the start of a critical fortune that has been described as "the longest and richest enjoyed by any poem written in a vernacular language."[14] In 1322, just a year after Dante died, his son Jacopo believed it was necessary to provide commentary that would help readers arrive at the Commedia's "deep and true meaning."[15] The list of fourteenth-century commentaries, which is truly staggering, includes such illustrious authors in their own regard as Boccaccio and Benvenuto da Imola.[16] The focused attention to individual words, lines, and themes in Dante by those early commentators continued the exegetical work of Dante himself and his own minute explications of the poetry of his Vita nuova, a crucial element in Dante's goal of establishing vernacular literature as worthy of the same amount of scholarly investment as revered Latin authors like Virgil, Ovid, and Horace.[17]

One does well to look beyond the facts and figures of Dante's earliest reception in trying to imagine what it was like, as a reader in the poet's own time, to confront a work of such surpassing strangeness and originality as the Commedia. Simply put, there was nothing like it before—or, one might well argue, since. There were certainly traditional epics, especially the Aeneid (19 BCE) from Dante's guide Virgil, who sang of the founding of Rome and the wars waged on behalf of its self-assumed imperial mission. There were also lesser instances of the genre, like Statius's Thebaid (c. 80–90 CE), a story of the struggle for the throne in the Greek city of Thebes, as well as a host of other epics now largely forgotten or lost to time. And there were of course the famous Homeric epics that few in medieval Italy (Dante not excepted) could read in their original Greek.[18] Finally, there were more personal, spiritual works like Augustine's Confessions and many other texts, ranging from Thomas of

Celano's hagiographic *Vita beati Francisci* (The life of blessed Francis, 1228) to Saint Bonaventure's *Itinerarium mentis in Deum* (The mind's journey to God, 1258–59), which celebrated in their individual ways the same Christian spirit that had so enraptured Dante.

But to grasp the impact of Dante's *Commedia* on its first Italian readers, we need to take a more granular look at the works circulating alongside Dante's great poem. Of immediate relevance to Dante's initial reception was the class of poems that Dante himself had written in his earlier, Sweet New Style days: ravishing lyrics that told of love's inspirations, the physical maladies it caused, and its elevation of the courtly lover in lockstep with the devastations wrought by the unrequited feelings it induced. Two of the main poems of this genre, both profoundly influential to Dante, were Guido Guinizelli's "Al cor gentil rempaira sempre amore" ("Love always returns to the gentle heart," c. 1265–76) and Guido Cavalcanti's "Donna me prega" ("A lady bids me," c. 1295–1300). Though the poetry of the *Commedia* would be radically different from the Sweet New Style in important ways—its use of narrative, its wildly inventive lexicon, its mixing of high and low styles—it still continued to employ the language, metaphors, and themes of this earlier movement, especially at key moments. The reader accustomed to the Sweet New Style—the reader fluent, so to speak, in its language of love—would find its traces throughout the *Commedia*.

A second major contemporary branch of writing that would have prepared readers for the startling newness of the *Comedy* was the growing strand of what we might call proto-humanist work being done in the increasingly secular and intellectually sophisticated Italian centers of learning, especially Dante's own Florence. A prime example of this was a text written by one of the most memorable characters in all of *Inferno*, Dante's former

teacher and the renowned public intellectual and master of rhetoric, Brunetto Latini, who is condemned to run naked beneath
a hail of fiery rain in the Circle of the Sodomites in canto 15.
Indeed, if there was one medieval work that was closest in kinship to Dante's *Commedia*, it might well be Latini's *Li livres dou
trésor* (The book of treasures), written in French while Latini
was exiled in France (1261–68), where he also wrote an abridged
version of the text in Tuscan, *Il tesoretto* (The little treasure). An
encyclopedic consideration of history, philosophy, ethics, and
religion, Latini's project bears striking parallels to that of Dante.
It features a narrator, Latini himself, taught by a great Roman
poet (in this case Ovid, not Virgil), and it recounts a dreamlike
vision that even begins with its protagonist lost in a "strange
wood" (*selva diversa*).[19] On the surface, Latini's work seems
closer to the letter of Dante's *Commedia* than the more rarefied
and love-obsessed lyrics of the Sweet New Style. Yet *Il tesoretto*
lacks two ingredients that would drive Dante's early reception:
as poetry, it falls flat, its erudition far outweighing its literary
qualities, and linguistically, it offers little in the way of new and
inventive uses of the vernacular. Despite the distance Dante
would travel from the Sweet New Style, its lessons in how to
reinvent a vernacular literary tradition shaped Dante's agenda
in the *Commedia*, which is radically experimental from beginning to end. All this was not lost on his first readers. Ultimately,
the majesty and force of the *Commedia*, what made it an immediate cultural phenomenon even while Dante was living, derived
from its new approach to the question of what poetic language
could be.

To gauge how central the issue of Dante as vernacular poet
was to the early reception of the *Commedia*, it is best to turn to
the most influential reading of Dante in all of the fourteenth
century—and perhaps in all of the centuries to come. Dante had

the good fortune to have as his first biographer a writer whose gifts and fame almost rivaled his own: Giovanni Boccaccio. His *Decameron* (c. 1348–53) helped spawn much of what came to be associated with the Renaissance: its secularity, its celebration of human creativity, and its promotion of the aesthetic as an end in itself, among other qualities. Boccaccio was also one of the most important scholars in all of Europe, and throughout his career he often turned to the *Commedia*. In the early 1350s, he published the first draft of his *Trattatello in laude di Dante* (Little treatise in praise of Dante), a work that began the tradition of legendary lives, *vite*, that freely mixed fact and fiction in constructing their biographical monuments to Dante's genius.[20] According to Boccaccio, Dante's mother dreamt she was beneath a "lofty laurel tree," the symbol of poetry, where she delivered a son, "who in the shortest time, nourished only by the berries that fell from the laurel tree," transformed first into a shepherd and then a peacock.[21] Nothing less than the grace of God granted the Florentines Dante, "who was first to open the way for the return of the Muses, banished from Italy."[22] It is easy to smile at Boccaccio's excesses, but they mask a serious intent. By calling Dante the writer who restored the exiled muses, Boccaccio was signaling that it was first and foremost as a poet (*poeta*)—and as a *vernacular* poet—that Dante earned his claim to immortality. The message is clear: Boccaccio read Dante as Italy's first poet laureate, the man who redeemed its vernacular dialect, even though this medieval prince of letters would never be able to wear the actual crown, suffering as he had through a bitter two-decade exile. In reading Boccaccio's initial *vita*, one cannot help but think that Boccaccio himself is posthumously crowning his beloved subject.

The ironies of Boccaccio's symbolic laurel are considerable. He was far less generous toward Dante in the second version of his *Trattatello in laude di Dante* from the 1360s, fundamentally due to the influence of the towering figure who would actually receive the laurel crown on Rome's Capitoline Hill on April 8, 1341: Francesco Petrarca, alias Petrarch. The date of Petrarch's coronation fell on Easter Sunday, the anniversary of Dante's own journey through the afterworld. Even in Dante's death, the relation between the two always seemed to take on the trappings of rivalry.

If the history of Dante's early reception begins with Boccaccio, it ends with Petrarch, who became one of Boccaccio's closest friends as well as the most famous author of his day. It is tempting to think of Dante and Petrarch as two parallel lines within whose boundaries the entire history of Italian literature was to be written. Their surface similarities are as astonishing as the discrepancies that divide them: both were born to Florentine families that suffered exile, and Dante even met and was on friendly terms with Petrarch's father during this period of expulsion. A mere four decades separate their births, Dante in 1265 and Petrarch in 1304. And each would become a "father" or "crown" of Italian literature, Dante for his contributions to the Italian language and the vernacular epic, Petrarch for his scholarship and exquisite lyric poetry. In retrospect, it's clear that Dante stood between Petrarch and the title he yearned for above all others: greatest Italian writer of all time. Ironically— though once again fittingly—the issue that most divided Petrarch and Dante was the question of vernacular poetry.

In 1359, Boccaccio sent Petrarch a copy of the *Commedia* copied in his own hand, along with a collection of fifteen sonnets by Dante, the first edition of his own *Trattatello in laude di Dante*, and a Latin poem praising Petrarch as the savior of "Our Italy." Petrarch was none too pleased with the gift. "If my many concerns were not so pressing," he snapped, "I might even strive to the best of my powers to rescue [Dante]."[23] This initial rebuff was the start of a contempt that would become more wideranging. Petrarch went on to deride Dante as a mere "dialect" love poet, putting him in the same category as poetic mediocrities like Guittone d'Arezzo, a figure whom even Dante criticized in *Purgatorio* 24 as held back in a "knot" from the inspiration of the Sweet New Style.[24]

As we see in his tormented autobiographical work *Secretum* (My secret book, 1353), Petrarch could be supremely contentious, even neurotic, and his divided self is never more apparent than in this critique of Dante. He snobbishly looked down on Dante for that same vernacular lyricism that, as fate would have it, proved to be Petrarch's own ticket to literary immortality. Along with Boccaccio, Petrarch believed himself to be at the literary vanguard of what we now call Renaissance humanism in the form of a revival of interest in ancient literature, especially Latin, and a celebration of a subject hitherto scorned on religious grounds: pagan moral philosophy. The scholar in Petrarch recoiled at the thought of vernacular poetry and its popular appeal. His view influenced Boccaccio, who late in his career sympathized with Petrarch's derisive labeling of such everyday readers of the vernacular as "idiots in the tavern" (*ydiotas in tabernis*).[25] For Petrarch and for the elderly Boccaccio, literature was not for dolts immune to poetry's status as a "sacred and fixed science" with "eternal principles."[26]

Not that Petrarch devalued poetry per se. Fashioning himself as the Italic heir of Virgil, he spent much of his life working on the formidable Latin hexameter poem *Africa*, the story of the Second Punic War and the Roman general Scipio Africanus's defeat of the Carthaginian leader Hannibal. In Petrarch's eyes, this learned and classically inflected poetic text would be the antithesis of what he believed were the overly demotic and rough-hewn vernacular literary forms that Dante had dedicated his career to disseminating. Petrarch began work on *Africa* as a relatively young man, in 1338, and completed a draft in 1344. But he jealously guarded it and prevented it from circulating, refining and revising it up to his death in 1374. After a protracted struggle over the definitive version of the poem, it was not published until 1396–97. Whatever dreams the living Petrarch may have had about his poem's posthumous celebrity quickly dissolved in the fickle light of posterity. Though *Africa* enjoyed some early success, especially as a school text, it quickly faded into oblivion. Today, only the Petrarchan or Renaissance specialist has even heard of it.

But the occlusion of Petrarch's patently un-Dantesque *Africa* is more than made up for by the success of the work that would bring him enduring and, likely, endless fame: 366 vernacular love poems inspired by his muse, Laura, and collected into his *Canzoniere* (Songbook), which he labored over with the same intensity he devoted to his failed epic, from roughly 1327 to 1368. The difference was that these gorgeous, refined, and melancholic lyrics of love were done in secret, with the author dismissing them as "trifles" (*nugae*)—the same withering dismissal he reserved for Dante's vernacular poetry.[27] The elite scholar and Latinist in Petrarch could not conceive that such humble matter as his lyric poems to Laura, written in the dialect of his Tuscan homeland and on so common a theme as love, would propel him into the literary pantheon. Yet that is exactly what happened. In striking out against the "dialect" element in Dante, Petrarch was also unwittingly belittling the essence of his transcendent poetic greatness.

Tellingly, the original title of Petrarch's love poems was *Rerum vulgarium fragmenta*, which means literally "Fragments of common things," but which translates more accurately as

"Fragments composed in the vernacular." As the title suggests, Petrarch probed the local dialect's ability to capture everyday experience without reducing language to the unspectacular, clichéd, or uninspiring. So, just like Dante, Petrarch was invested in writing about the common in an uncommon way. But for him the act was somehow more shameful, less noble, than striving for more rarefied literary projects like his star-crossed *Africa*.

A small library of criticism has been written on Dante's influence on Petrarch and Boccaccio and on the larger issue of Dante's presence in the Italian literature of the fourteenth century.[28] Despite the undeniable impact of Boccaccio and Petrarch in shaping the afterlife of Dante in the first decades after his death, Dante's work reached a range of other readers outside of this elite perch. For one thing, the *Commedia* was copied, quite literally, into the legal codices and official documents of Italy's increasingly literate professional class—leaving us with the image of lawyers, scribes, and clerks daydreaming about Dante's verse while they presumably should have been focused on their paid duties.[29] Dante also became a character in prose works whose representation of the poet bore witness to his widespread celebrity. In Franco Sacchetti's *Three Hundred Tales*, a *Decameron*-like collection of short stories, Dante appears in various guises: in one story, he upbraids a blacksmith for not reciting his *Commedia* correctly; in another, he insults a garbage collector for the same sin of mispronouncing his work; and in a third, a scandalous poet takes refuge in a church and swears that the *Commedia*, though written by a mere mortal, is superior to the Bible.

We have seen how the responses to Dante's *Commedia* in the 1300s occurred in a wide range of cultural contexts and socioeconomic levels. That the vernacular was a defining element of

Dante's early reception is entirely fitting. For Dante had carefully and methodically orchestrated his efforts on behalf of the *volgare* from the start of his career, beginning in the earliest poems of the *Vita nuova* and continuing into the majestic verse of the *Commedia*. To comprehend the scope of this vernacular Dante, we might jump ahead six centuries, to when Italy was still technically without a unifying language—and without a unifying state—as it had been in Dante's time. In 1827, Alessandro Manzoni published the first edition of his legendary *I promessi sposi* (The betrothed), often called Italy's first modern novel, in a mix of his native Lombard and elements from other Italian dialects, including Dante's Tuscan. By the mid-nineteenth century, as Italy struggled toward political and linguistic unification, Manzoni sensed that a dramatic cultural contribution was needed. So he decided to translate—actually, *auto*-translate—his novel into the second Tuscan edition that appeared in 1840. In recognition of his efforts, which helped elevate Tuscan to the national language of Italy upon unification in 1861, King Vittorio Emanuele II named Manzoni honorary senator and assigned him presidency of the commission for the unification of the Italian language. The force motivating Manzoni's efforts on behalf of the dialect was clear: in his own words, he had gone to "rinse the laundry in Florence's Arno River" (*risciacquare i panni in Arno*), his maxim for traveling to the verbal land of Dante. So Dante's efforts on behalf of the vernacular had not only conditioned the first responses to the *Commedia* but had also helped create the language of the newborn Italian nation.

Chapter 2

Comedìa Proibita

WHEN THE DOMINICAN friar Guido Vernani infamously dubbed Dante a demonic "vessel" in 1327—that is, seductive on the surface but poisonous within—he was not alone. Though many early readers celebrated Dante's work, especially his efforts on behalf of the vernacular, others found his religious beliefs dangerous and his idiosyncratic view of the afterlife a threat to the same spiritual salvation that the *Commedia* aimed to espouse. This early fate of the *Commedia* was ironic in the extreme: Dante had celebrated Vernani's Dominicans for their intellectual rigor, embodied in their "holy athlete" (*santo atleta*) and founder, Saint Dominic, in *Paradiso* 12. In fact, the extended sequence in *Paradiso* 11–12, which contains biographies of both Dominic and Francis, represents a key moment in Dante's religious vision. The story of Dominic's life is narrated by Bonaventure, a mystic from the Franciscan order whose work *The Mind's Journey to God* spoke of how humankind could love and contemplate God through the examples of Christ and Francis. Meanwhile, the brilliant medieval Scholastic and Dominican Aquinas, Dante's prime source for the theological discourses of *Paradiso*, told the story of the "poor little one" (*poverello*), Francis, founder of the Franciscan order and a Christian renowned for his emotional connection to God. This celebrated chiasmus, where each saintly life is recounted by a member of a rival religious order, suggests how Dante's Paradiso harmonizes differing belief systems that coalesce in their mutual love of the one Christian God.[1] So the rejection of the Commedia by a Dominican order elevated to intellectual and spiritual prominence in Paradiso would certainly have stung Dante. In truth, Dante had much more in common with the deeply cerebral and analytically incisive Dominic than he did with the naïve, nature-loving Francis. But Vernani's assault on Dante was only the first in a series of religious battles faced by the Commedia.

Vernani was born toward the end of the thirteenth century in Rimini, the city of Dante's doomed lovers, Paolo and Francesca. He passionately defended the temporal power of the Catholic Church, a position he outlined in his commentary on the Unam sanctam (One holy church, 1302), a papal bull from Dante's mortal enemy Pope Boniface VIII, the man responsible for Dante's exile. Written between 1312 and 1315, Dante's De monarchia (On monarchy) implicitly critiques the principles of the Unam sanctam, which argued for complete submission to papal supremacy and the priority of the Church's spiritual power in the secular realm. Dante's rejection of the authority expressed in Boniface's treatise set Vernani on a literary counteroffensive. His De reprobatione "Monarchiae" compositae a Dante (Refutation of the "Monarchia" composed by Dante, 1327–34), written soon after the condemnation of Dante's political thinking by Cardinal Bertrando del Poggetto in 1328, attacked Dante's impassioned defense in De monarchia of a world dictatorship that was to be split evenly between the temporal domain, headed by a holy Roman emperor in the mold of Dante's ill-fated Henry VII, and the spiritual realm, led by the pope.[2]

Dante's political stance permeates Marco Lombardo's famous speech about the "two suns" in *Purgatorio* 16:

"For Rome, which made the world good, used to have
two suns; and they made visible two paths—
the world's path and the pathway that is God's.
Each has eclipsed the other; now the sword
has joined the shepherd's crook; the two together
must of necessity result in evil,
because, so joined, one need not fear the other:
and if you doubt me, watch the fruit and flower,
for every plant is known by what it seeds."

"*Soleva Roma, che 'l buon mondo feo,
due soli aver, che l'una e l'altra strada
facean vedere, e del mondo e di Deo.
L'un l'altro ha spento; ed è giunta la spada
col pasturale, e l'un con l'altro insieme
per viva forza mal convien che vada;
però che, giunti, l'un l'altro non teme:
se non mi credi, pon mente a la spiga,
ch'ogn' erba si conosce per lo seme.*" (106–14)

Coming just after a key passage on free will, Marco's metaphor of the "two suns" sets the emperor and pope as equals, revising a dominant trope in the political theory of Dante's time, which had the pope as the sun and the emperor as a contingent moon, deriving his light from the more powerful pontiff.[3] The concluding words of *De monarchia* cloak the message of Marco Lombardo's poetic imagery in full ideological garb, as they feature a mutually reinforcing flow of light from the spiritual to the temporal order and vice versa:

Let Caesar therefore show that reverence towards Peter which a firstborn son should show his father, so that, illumined by the light of paternal grace, he may the more effectively light up the world, over which he has been placed by Him alone who is ruler over all things spiritual and temporal. (3.16.18)

Vernani was as unmoved by Dante's poetics as he was by his politics. His "reading" of *De monarchia*—if one can call it that— was a pure hatchet job, beginning with his dedication:

Among the devil's other vessels, there was, indeed, a certain individual who wrote many fantastic things in poetry, a pa- laverous sophist, pleasing many through his eloquence with its hollow words; one who, using his poetical phantasms and fictions and, in the words of Philosophy as she consoled Bo- ethius, bringing whores onto the stage with their sweet, siren songs, fraudulently seduces not only sick minds, but even zealous ones, to the destruction of salutary truth.[4]

With florid takedowns like "palaverous sophist," Vernani exudes a contempt so all-consuming that he cannot even bring himself to name Dante. He blasts the unmentioned *Commedia* as a work of "poetical phantasms and fictions" that camouflages its insidious messages in deceptively lovely garb. Ironically enough, for Vernani the poem was a "siren's song," similar to what Dante himself excoriates in the second Purgatorial dream in canto 19, when the intoxicating siren-like figure who appears to him in his sleep is gutted by a saintly lady and is revealed to be a foul and noxious hag. Vernani assumes the mantle of a purifying spirit similar in ferocity to the lady who rends the false bearer of aesthetic images to protect the dreaming Dante.

After his sidelong condemnation of the *Commedia*, Vernani moves to the purpose of his tract: censuring *De monarchia*, a work he describes as "specious, yet somewhat methodical . . . all the while mixing many lies with occasional truths."[5] Vernani seems to respect or fear Dante's rhetorical skill while reviling the content of his work and its "spurious colors and deceitful figures of truth and honesty [that contain] a poison [that is] deadly and pestilential."[6] Though Vernani accepts Dante's premise of a single, sovereign imperial ruler in the *Monarchia*—and thus by extension in the *Commedia*—he criticizes the poet's methods. While Dante proposed that it is "beneficial for the world to have one single monarch," Vernani writes, "a foolish love of his own opinion obscured his wits and our writer was unable to discover who the true monarch was."[7] The gist of Vernani's critique then emerges: in promoting a world ruler to govern the lives of men and control the secular destiny of humankind, Dante advocated removing power from the supreme religious leader, the pope, whom many (including Vernani) believed should hold sway in the earthly as well as in the spiritual sphere.

Vernani's criticism recalls why many within Dante's own Guelph faction parted ways with him. Though the Guelphs in general advocated for the temporal power of the papacy, many within the party (Dante among them) wanted to circumscribe that power out of fear that the papacy was becoming too influential in Florentine politics. This situation played out with devastating consequences for Dante in the early 1300s, when supporters of Pope Boniface VIII, Florence's Black Guelphs led by Corso Donati, succeeded in outmaneuvering Dante and the anti-Boniface White Guelphs, resulting in the detention of Dante in Rome in 1301 while he was on a diplomatic mission to the papal court. It was not long before Dante was pronounced guilty of corruption and exiled from Florence, on pain of death, in 1302.

Vernani couched the matter of Dante's rejection of papal power in Christological terms. "The prince of the world," he wrote, "is the supreme pontiff of the Christians, the universal vicar of Jesus Christ," adding, "if all men obeyed according to the law of the Gospels handed down by Christ, there would exist the most perfect monarchy in the world."[8] In a statement that directly contradicted Dante's separation of absolute power into temporal and spiritual realms, Vernani argued, "Never was there in the world any true monarch except for [the pope], as I have clearly proved by reasoning and authority in my treatise *On Papal Power*; and that no other power is necessary among men as I have clearly demonstrated in the same place."[9]

Vernani censured another bulwark of Dante's political views in *De monarchia*: his reverence for pagan culture, which also permeates the *Commedia*.[10] The second part of Vernani's treatise sought to debunk each of Dante's reasons for justifying Roman imperial power. He begins by accusing the ancient Romans, in tendentious fashion, of "worship of demons," cherry-picking sources ranging from Saint Paul to Saint Augustine.[11] However dubious, Vernani's channeling of the medieval animus toward the Latin world represented a major grievance felt by many contemporaries toward Dante. Augustine himself had pointed out the incompatibility between the life of a good Christian and the love for Latin literature, a connection that is quite evident in Dante. In his *Confessions*, Augustine described how, since childhood, he had been so passionate about ancient books that it became an obsession, still another earthly attachment fueling his spiritual pain. So he decided to renounce his favorite author, Virgil, vowing never again to read his epic *Aeneid* and its story of tragic love between the Trojan prince Aeneas and the Carthaginian queen Dido, who kills herself when Aeneas abandons her:

> What is more pitiable than a wretch without pity for himself who weeps over the death of Dido dying for love of Aeneas,

but not weeping over himself dying for his lack of love for you, my God, light of my heart, bread of the inner mouth of my soul.[12]

By echoing such Church fathers as Augustine in critiquing Dante's love of pagan culture, Vernani struck a chord that likely resonated with fellow prelates.

Dante's admiration for Virgilian epic encompassed his reverence for the political power of the ancient Roman people, which he believed held the key for reuniting the divided inhabitants of the fragmented Italian peninsula during his own era. *De monarchia* aimed to show that ancient Rome's ascent to power was divinely sanctioned, a position that infuriated Vernani. Drawing a parallel between the legal foundation of the Roman Empire and the transcendent justice that led God to punish Adam for his original sin, Dante argued that no transgression may be punished without an all-powerful judge whose wisdom and authority far surpass that of any individual human. This notion drew an enraged response from Vernani: "Here the wretch [Dante] reached the heights of his delirium: as he raised his mouth to heaven, his tongue lolled along the ground. Who ever made such a disgraceful error as to say that the punishment due for original sin lay in the power of any earthly judge?"[13] Here as elsewhere, Vernani's ire was incited by Dante's desire to grant to the secular ruler an authority equal to the pontiff's. Refuting this claim with biblical references, Vernani argued that "Christ gave Peter and Paul's successors the power of judicial discipline over all his sheep. Ergo, the pope may chastise the emperor, who is one among Christ's sheep."[14]

Despite Dante's belief in the power of the papacy in the spiritual realm, certain popes receive harsh judgments in the *Commedia*. A dominant motif in Dante's antipapal attitude is his loathing for the avidity of popes who enriched themselves through the corrupt use of their offices. In *Inferno* 19, Dante punishes the sin of simony, the selling of church favors named after Simon Magus, who had tried to buy his way into apostolic power.[15] Approaching the sinners who lie entombed in fire, Dante meets Pope Nicholas III, whose cocktail of greed and nepotism is advertised in his words to Dante:

> "and surely [I] was a son of the she-bear,
> so eager to advance the cubs that
> pursed wealth above while here I purse myself."
>
> *"e veramente fui figliuol de l'orsa,*
> *cupido sì per avanzar li orsatti,*
> *che sù l'avere e qui me misi in borsa."* (70–72)

As has been noted,[16] Dante's direct attack on Nicholas III serves as an indirect encounter with his mortal enemy, Pope Boniface VIII, as Nicholas mistakes Dante for Boniface, leading him to cry out:

> ... "Are you already standing,
> already standing there, o Boniface?
>
> . . .
>
> Are you so quickly sated with the riches
> for which you did not fear to take by guile
> the Lovely Lady, then to violate her?"
>
> ... *"Se' tu già costì ritto,*
> *se' tu già costì ritto, Bonifazio?*
>
> . . .
>
> *Se' tu sì tosto di quell' aver sazio*
> *per lo qual non temesti tòrre a 'nganno*
> *la bella donna, e poi di farne strazio?"* (52–53, 55–57)

The *Commedia* takes place in April 1300, and Boniface would not die till October of 1303. But Dante's premature condemnation of him issues from so personal a hatred that, in the words of one commentator, it led him to set "aside the theology of repentance, which holds that sinners can delay repentance until the very last moment of life and still be saved."[17]

Such ad hominem attacks against Vernani's beloved papal authority could never escape his counterfire. "When [Dante] says that the Church cannot hold earthly possessions and did not have the power to accept them [*Mon.* 3:10], he speaks in ignorance, failing to understand either what he says or what he affirms," Vernani writes.[18] Defending the accumulation of wealth as necessary both to establish the presence of the Christian Church and to redistribute the offerings it receives back to the poor, Vernani protests that he was "amazed that that presumptuous person failed to keep in mind that holy martyrs, confessors, and especially the holy doctors, Augustine, Ambrose, and Gregory, held, maintained and increased the earthly wealth of their churches.... Nor would they have done this either against God or against conscience."[19] Vernani rejected Dante's dichotomy between spiritual and temporal power by affirming that "among the people of God, God himself ordained the temporal power through the power of his priests."[20] For Vernani, as for Boniface VIII, all were subject to the word of God and His earthly representative, the pope.

All told, Vernani's *Refutation of the "Monarchia" Composed by Dante* is an odd text. As Anthony Cassell aptly describes it, Vernani's contempt for Dante trapped him in a polemical stance that bordered on the propagandistic and led to a fast and loose approach to the facts:

> . . . Vernani's dogged obsessions, his show of high-handed self-complacency, his purblind self-righteousness, his adamant

parti-pris, and his determination to show no quarter betray ulterior motives and ultimate frustration. Perhaps to nudge approval from his superiors, either real or socially imagined, he resorts overmuch to humorless mockery [of Dante's *De monarchia*]. Even though the friar apparently kept his own copy of the Refutation with him in his cell at San Cataldo in Rimini until his death . . . he left his treatise, in fact, unpolished and unadorned, bereft of limned capital letters, petering out flaccidly without summation and allowing many chapters of Dante's most persuasive reasonings to go unanswered.[21]

Vernani's interpretation of Dante may not have been accurate, but it was effective: after its ban by the Dominican Order in the fourteenth century, *De monarchia* in its entirety was placed on the pope's dreaded Index Librorum Prohibitorum (Index of forbidden books) from 1554 to 1881.[22]

Vernani's criticism of Dante compels us to ask where and how Dante did—and did not—fit into the religious discourses of his day. As Peter Hawkins argues, though Dante's *Commedia* has in many respects "set the gold standard" in the Western tradition for religious poetry, it has also troubled clerical readers because of its unorthodox views, which include mingling "pagan worthies with unbaptized infants—the only souls the Church meant to be there [in Limbo]."[23] Hawkins goes on to name other controversial positions, such as Dante's making his muse Beatrice, a Florentine noblewoman of no recorded religious virtues, the divine mediatrix of his journey through the afterworld and a close collaborator with the Virgin Mary.[24]

The most concrete resistance to Dante's poetry on religious grounds came a few centuries after Vernani's attack, during the Spanish Inquisition. A tribunal court system established in 1478 by Ferdinand II and Isabella to maintain Catholic orthodoxy

within the Spanish Kingdom, the Inquisition created the Index
of Forbidden Books to combat heretical ideas that allegedly
endangered moral life and threatened the precepts of Roman
Catholicism. While initially intended to censure entire books,
the Inquisition quickly realized that this would have the unwanted effect of depressing literacy levels within their ranks. So
they opted instead for redacting unwanted parts of otherwise
acceptable texts. Dante's *Commedia* was one of these works to
undergo moral surgery: no Christian should read it until it was
cleansed of its notional sins.

Such was the fate of an edition of the *Commedia* from 1564,
published by the Sessa family in Venice (Figure 1). This magnificent edition of Dante, which contains commentaries by
eminent Renaissance *dantisti* including Cristoforo Landino,
ended up in Arévalo, Spain, where a zealous Spanish cleric sanctioned by the Holy See set about purifying the poem of passages at odds with Catholic doctrine. His redactions included
passages from *Inferno* 11.7–9, where Dante describes the heresy
of Pope Anastasius, and *Paradiso* 9.136–42, verses that excoriate
the confluence of money, greed, and corruption that Dante believed was ruining the papacy.[25]

A key moment of censorship occurs, not surprisingly, in
Dante's most infamously anti-papal canto, *Inferno* 19:

"You, shepherds, the Evangelist had noticed
when he saw her who sits upon the waters
and realized she fornicates with kings,
she who was born with seven heads and had
the power and support of the ten horns,
as long as virtue was her husband's pleasure.
You've made yourselves a god of gold and silver;
how are you different from idolaters,

FIGURE 1. Cover page of the censored edition of the *Commedia*, published in Venice, 1564. From Robert D. Farber University Archives and Special Collections, Brandeis University.

save that they worship one and you a hundred?
Ah, Constantine, what wickedness was born—
and not from your conversion—from the dower
that you bestowed upon the first rich father!"

"Di voi pastor s'accorse il Vangelista,
quando colei che siede sopra l'acque
puttaneggiar coi regi a lui fu vista;
quella che con le sette teste nacque,
e da le diece corna ebbe argomento,
fin che virtute al suo marito piacque.
Fatto v'avete dio d'oro e d'argento;
e che altro è da voi a l'idolatre,
se non ch'elli uno, e voi ne orate cento?
Ahi, Costantin, di quanto mal fu matre,
non la tua conversion, ma quella dote
che da te prese il primo ricco patre!" (106–17)

Dante's vicious critique of prelates who worship "gold and silver," expressed in the sexual rhetoric of a Vatican that "fornicates" with kings, was an obvious target for the Inquisition. The
censor redacted the above passage with ink that has thankfully
faded over the centuries, revealing the original text it had once
obscured (Figure 2). The Holy See's official approval of the censorship is clear from the original document pasted on the back
of the title page and signed by one of the Inquisitors approving
the cancellations. The message, translated from the original
Spanish, reads: "Arévalo, Spain, on April 16, 1614, this book has
been purged in accordance with the Expurgatory Catalogue of
Don Fernando de Riezas, Head Inquisitor; so empowered by
the Commission of the Holy Office. . . ." (Figure 3).[26]
    Another Venetian edition of the *Commedia* suffered a similar
fate. A volume published by Bernardino Stagnino in 1512, again

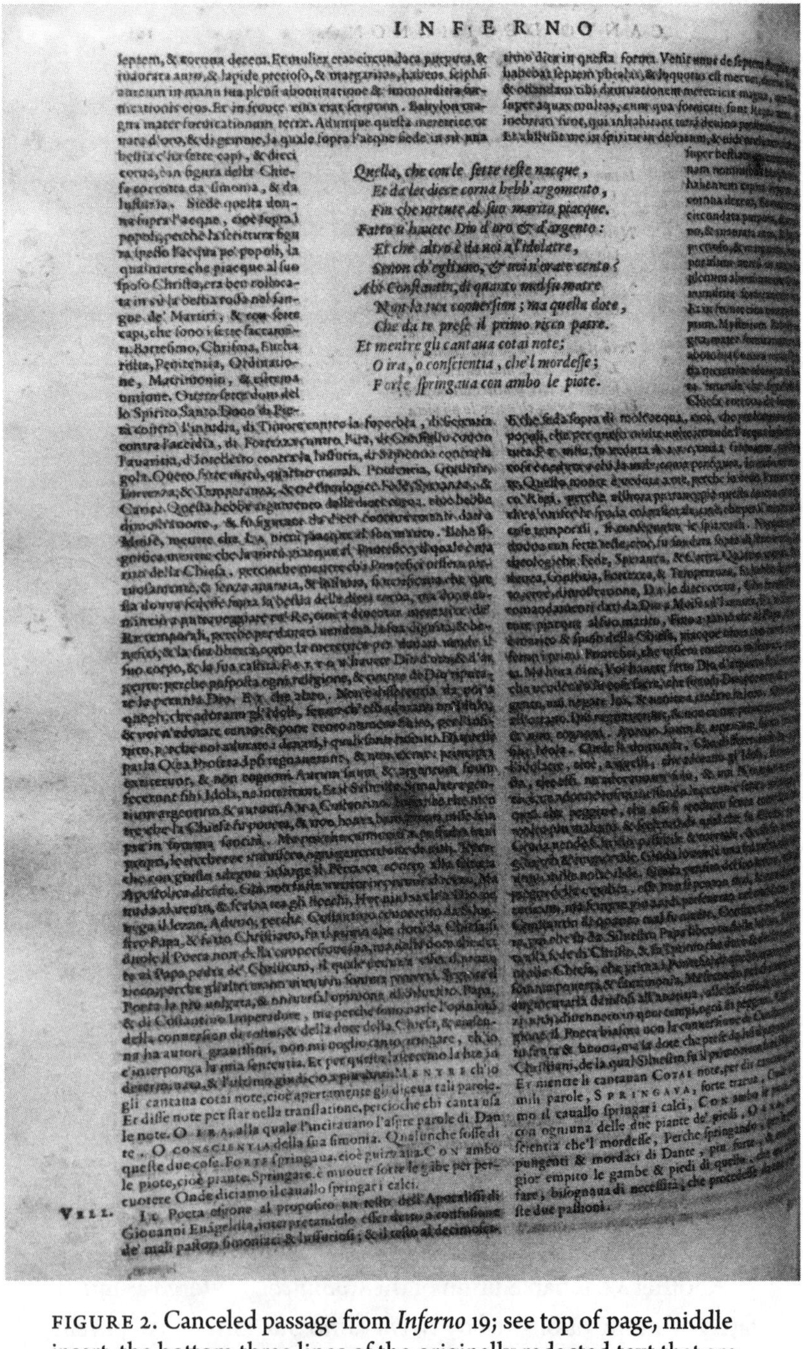

Quella, che con le sette teste nacque,
  Et da le diece corna hebb' argomento,
  Fin che uirtute al suo marito piacque.
Fatto v'hauete Dio d'oro & d'argento:
  Et che altra è da noi à l'idolatre,
  Senon ch'egli uno, & uoi n'orate cento?
Ahi Constantin, di quanto mal fu matre,
  Non la tua conuersion; ma quella dote,
  Che da te prese il primo ricco patre.
Et mentre gli cantaua cotai note;
  O ira, o conscientia, che'l mordesse;
  Forse springaua con ambo le piote.

FIGURE 2. Canceled passage from *Inferno* 19; see top of page, middle insert, the bottom three lines of the originally redacted text that are once again visible. Robert D. Farber University Archives and Special Collections, Brandeis University.

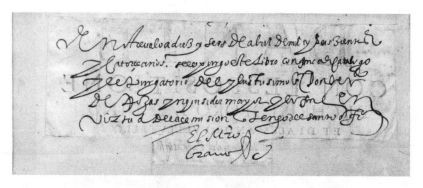

FIGURE 3. Handwritten approval of the redactions by the Spanish Inquisitor. From Robert D. Farber University Archives and Special Collections, Brandeis University.

with a commentary by Landino, found its way to Spain in the late 1500s, where it caught the disapproving eye of the Inquisition. The title page (Figure 4) ominously declares, "With commission from the Señores Inquisitors cross out and erase what is prohibited in this book" (*Con comisión de los S[eñor]es Inquisidores teste y borre lo prohibido deste libro*), followed by "[E]stevan Joan Velasco Vicario de S[ain]t Nicolás."[27] The volume contains many redacted passages, especially in Landino's commentary. In some places, an offending line is simply crossed out in ink, while longer passages have been papered over (Figure 5). The Inquisition was heavy-handed, imperious, and anti-intellectual when it came to the *Commedia*—and also consistent: many of the same passages redacted in the Venetian Sessa volume from 1564, especially Dante's attack on the rapacious popes from *Inferno* 19, were also expurgated from this earlier Stagnino edition from 1512.

Dante's *Commedia* was not his only work punished by the Church. Though it was no surprise that his controversial *De monarchia* was also placed in the Index, so was—remarkably enough—Dante's youthful autobiography of love and poetic apprenticeship, the *Vita nuova*. Inquisitorial censors altered

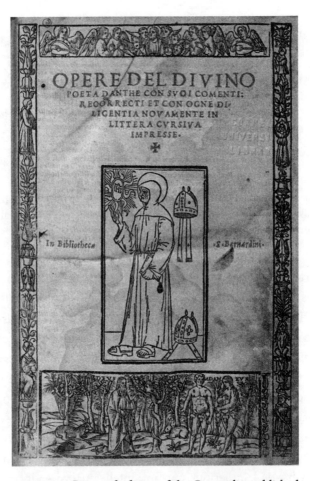

FIGURE 4. Censored edition of the *Commedia*, published in Venice, 1512. From Division of Rare and Manuscript Collections, Cornell University Library: Fiske Dante Collection.

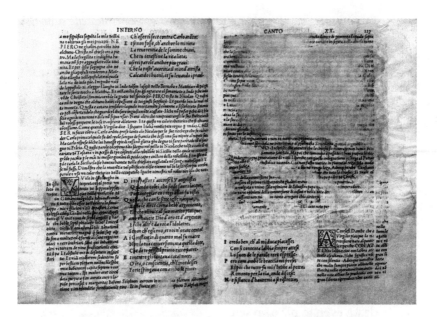

FIGURE 5. A severely redacted section of *Inferno* 19 containing Dante's attack against the Simoniac papacy. From Kenneth Spencer Research Library, University of Kansas.

or suppressed terms applied by Dante to Beatrice in the *editio princeps* of the *Vita nuova*, published in Florence in 1576.[28] The official sanction of the text is evidenced by this notice affixed to it by the Inquisitor:

> This *Vita nuova* by Dante was reviewed, along with the biography of this same Dante by Giovanni Boccaccio, and license is hereby granted to publish these works after the last day of December 1575. Brother Francesco da Pisa Min. Conu. The Inquisitor General of Florence.
>
> *Si è veduto la Vita Nuova descritta da Dante Allighieri, insieme con la Vita dell' istesso Dante descritta da Giouaun Boccaccio, e si è concesso licenzia che si stampino questo dì ultimo di*

Dicembre 1575 da Pisa Min. Conu. Inquisitor Generale dello stato di Fiorenza.[29]

In terms of religious doctrine, the original text of the *Vita nuova* seems harmless enough, and the redactions, from our modern perspective, come across as arbitrary and unnecessary: its anodyne allusions to God and descriptions of Beatrice as *gloriosa* all fell under the censor's malign scrutiny. As Paget Toynbee has shown, there were also redactions of a more serious nature. For example, at the beginning of Chapter 22, the censor replaced Dante's sentence

> *Siccome piacque al glorioso Sire, lo quale non nega la morte a se.*

> Just as pleased the glorious Lord Jesus, who did not deny death even to his own self.

with the much different:

> *Siccome piacque a quel vivace amore, il quale impresse questo affetto in me.*

> Just as pleased that lively love, which had such an effect on me.[30]

Some of the beautiful touches of the *Vita nuova* were also cut: in Chapter 23, the angels' original chant, "Hosannah in the highest" (*Osanna in excelsis*), is replaced by elliptical dots. Most grievously of all, in the dramatic conclusion of the *Vita nuova*, when Dante expresses his wish to remain silent about Beatrice until he can do her full justice with his writing, the sentence that originally read:

> And may it please Him, the Lord of courtesy, that my soul may turn to see the glory of his lady, that is that blessed Beatrice,

who gloriously looks into the face of Him who is blessed for all centuries. Amen.

E poi piaccia a Colui, che e Sire della cortesia, che la mia anima se ne possa gire a vedere la gloria della sua donna, cioè di quella benedetta Beatrice, la quale gloriosamente mira nella faccia di Colui qui est per omnia saecula benedictus. Amen.

is eviscerated into:

And may it please Him, who is the Lord of courtesy, that my soul may turn to see the glory of Him, who is blessed for all centuries.[31]

E poi piaccia a Colui, che è Sire della cortesia, che la mia anima se ne possa gire e vedere la gloria di Colui, qui est per omnia saecula benedictus.

The reference to Beatrice has been excised—and, with it, all the emotional resonance of the passage. The Inquisition did more than scrub the *Vita nuova* of many of its religious references; it crushed much of its poetry.

Despite these unfortunate episodes of Inquisitorial censorship, many of Dante's deviations from Christian doctrine went untouched in the first centuries after his death. As Barolini points out, "the Church on the whole . . . was willing to bracket Dante as a poet, a maker of *fictio*."[32] She goes on to say that the subsequent dichotomy between Dante as "poet" and "theologian" was institutionalized because commentators wanted "to keep poets safely bracketed from prophets (and especially a poet who complicated matters still further by deploying his poetic gifts in anything but prudent fashion, for instance by invoking classical models [alongside] biblical ones)."[33] These words are worth bearing in mind as we continue to chart the afterlife of the *Commedia* through both its secular and spiritual trajectories. As we will see, Vernani's caustic words would be recast in new forms by new voices that, like the Dominican friar, often took issue with Dante's idiosyncratic approach to questions of the soul. Similarly, the separation between Dante *poeta* and *theologus*, a critical maneuver rejected by Barolini, would lead many of Dante's readers to see him as a poet whose power derived, paradoxically, from his ability to transcend the same religious matters that constitute the essence of his poem.

Chapter 3

Renaissance Visions

IN THE FIRST CENTURY of responses to the *Commedia*, a refrain went that Dante's bold decision to write in the language of his hometown had initiated a new chapter in literary history. Dante's efforts on behalf of the vernacular were infused with a parallel desire to render biblical and religious discourse accessible to broad swaths of readers, in the manner of the humble speech (*sermo humilis*) studied by Erich Auerbach. This process incurred huge risks, as the more scholarly—Petrarch foremost among them—criticized Dante for his raw and supposedly inelegant style. Similarly, more doctrinally minded prelates—typified to the extreme by Guido Vernani—rose to question, and often to condemn, his highly personal religious choices.

But sometimes resistance to the *Commedia* had a paradoxically positive effect on Dante's legacy. Because of its obvious bias and lack of philological rigor, Vernani's critique found few adherents outside of the Dominican Order. And by and large the only other major religious censure of the *Commedia* came, unsurprisingly, during the Spanish Inquisition, a time of wholesale attacks on freedom of expression that were of course not limited to Dante. Meanwhile, Petrarch's personal animus against Dante and his vernacular love poetry helped make the *Commedia* an ongoing site of cultural debate throughout the historical epoch that would become a veritable synonym for Petrarch himself: the Renaissance. This is not to say that Dante remained the notional king of literary Italy during that era, as he had in the Middle Ages: the laurel crown had passed to Petrarch's head, both literally and metaphorically. Though later historians, most notably Jacob Burckhardt, would view Dante as the most important figure in the transition from the Middle Ages to the Renaissance, during the actual years of the Renaissance the term *Petrarchism* (and not *Dantism*) became a model for the refined, rules-based, and antiquity-oriented verse of elite authors ranging from Pierre Ronsard, Joachim Du Bellay, and Louise Labé in France to Edmund Spenser, Thomas Wyatt, and even William Shakespeare in England, among others.[1] Dante certainly remained vital to the cultural conversation during the European Renaissance, especially in Italy and his native Florence.[2] But in Europe as a whole, the elegant lyrics of Petrarch and not the deeply religious, occasionally crude language of Dante carried the day.

Indeed, Renaissance readers increasingly wondered where the *Commedia* belonged in the literary pantheon. Even Boccaccio, who transitioned from the young, daring author who wrote openly about sex and ridiculed the Church into an elder statesman of humanist letters who composed learned tracts in Latin in the manner of his *maître à penser* Petrarch, hesitated when the city of Florence offered him a prestigious and lucrative public lectureship on the *Commedia* in 1373. Boccaccio's literary audience by this point consisted mainly of fellow scholars. Long gone were the days when his scandalous writing from the *Decameron*—which included tales about a hardened criminal on his deathbed who tricks a gullible priest into thinking he is a saint, an arrogant horse dealer duped by a prostitute pretending to be his sister, and a group of nuns who discreetly employ a gardener to satisfy their carnal urges—could appeal to more popular audiences. The Latin humanist in him seriously doubted the Florentine public's ability to appreciate either Dante's poem or his learned expositions on it. He finally relented and accepted the position, most likely because he needed the money. But the lectures were cut short at only *Inferno* 17 because of Boccaccio's terminal illness; he died just a year after the start of his series, bringing the grand project to an abrupt end.

A split was developing in Florentine culture that would play itself out throughout Italy and Europe: Dante's *Commedia* continued to be read and celebrated among both popular and educated audiences. But at the upper echelons of literary society—and among many of the age's religious thinkers—criticisms of Dante's experimental and anticlerical writing raised doubts. Even among the more measured of these literary humanists, like the luminous Florentine chancellor Leonardo Bruni, a certain coolness toward Dante could be felt. Like many in his age and afterward, Bruni compared Dante to Petrarch, and the verdict came out in favor of the latter. "Petrarch was more wise and prudent [than Dante] in choosing the quiet and leisurely life than in working in the Republic and in disputes and civic factions," Bruni wrote, "for these often lead to one's being driven out by the wickedness of men and ingratitude of the people, as happened to Dante."[3] No shrinking violet, Petrarch would have agreed with Bruni's assessment. He once boasted to Boccaccio that, though Dante was Italy's finest philosopher, he was its number one poet—with poor Boccaccio a distant third as its ranking Christian.

The form the responses to Dante took was just as important as their message. Whereas Petrarch may have commanded more respect and prestige in literary circles, other groups, especially the age's visual artists, adored Dante. Illustrated editions of his *Commedia* exploded in number during the Renaissance. After the advent of the printing press in Germany around 1440, the *Commedia* emerged as the text of choice for many artists, building on the already vibrant tradition of illuminated manuscripts of Dante's work. The aesthetic splendor of this "visual Dante" had a long legacy, beginning with the magnificent Chantilly manuscript created in Pisa around 1345, the first complete illustration of Dante's text (Figure 6).[4]

As one might expect, the painters, sculptors, and architects from Dante's own Florence, many of whom would go on to become the most celebrated names in all of the Renaissance, were deeply taken with Dante's poem. A catalogue of the age's finest creators can sound like a local chapter of a Dante society: Filippo Brunelleschi, Sandro Botticelli, Leonardo da Vinci, Michelangelo Buonarotti, among many others, were committed *dantisti* in their individual ways. Some memorized patches of the *Commedia*, sprinkling references to it in their notebooks and conversations (Brunelleschi); others illustrated the entire poem (Botticelli); others, according to legend, may even have engaged in live "Dante contests" to see who could speak more insightfully about key passages in the *Commedia* (Leonardo, Michelangelo).[5] The reasons for Dante's pull on these creators were legion. To start with, he wrote in the vernacular that many of these unschooled, unlettered artists—few had studied Latin, the age's equivalent of a college degree—used themselves. And like Dante, some of them had moved on from their Florentine roots to international celebrity. Finally, Dante wrote in an earthy, accessible manner that appealed to these hard-living, prank-loving creatives. All told, Dante's Renaissance ghost was welcomed with open arms in the world of the Renaissance artistic workshop (*bottega*).

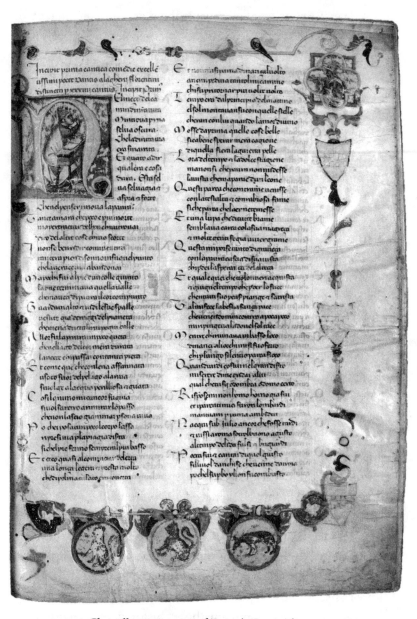

FIGURE 6. Chantilly manuscript of Dante's *Commedia*, c. 1345. From Chantilly, Musée Condé, Bibliothèque.

A deep dive into what is arguably the most consequential of all Renaissance visual responses to the *Commedia*, Botticelli's illustrated cycle of the poem, offers a striking example of what Dante's epic had come to represent in the fifteenth century.[6] Botticelli first began to illustrate the *Commedia* around 1481, when he was commissioned by Lorenzo di Pierfrancesco de' Medici, cousin of Lorenzo il Magnifico, to produce a deluxe edition of all one hundred cantos of the text. That same year, the Florentine government also commissioned a second special edition of the *Commedia*, the first ever printed in Florence. It was to be edited by the accomplished humanist Landino, who had tutored the city's golden children, Lorenzo il Magnifico and brother Giuliano de' Medici. The first nineteen cantos of *Inferno* in Landino's edition were visually based—rather maladroitly[7]— on drawings that Botticelli had created for Lorenzo di Pierfrancesco's deluxe private volume.[8]

The story of this volume turned out to be anything but straightforward. Botticelli would spend nearly fifteen years on it, till about the time of the invasion of Florence by King Charles VIII in 1494, the event that led to the dramatic rise and fall of Lorenzo di Pierfrancesco, who was ultimately expelled from Florence after briefly gaining traction as one of the city's most powerful men. Botticelli ended up illustrating almost all one hundred cantos, but many are in sparse, incomplete form, mainly sketches; only a few have any color at all. The deluxe volume may have been given to King Charles VIII by Lorenzo di Pierfrancesco as a diplomatic gift—there is no way of knowing for sure. For the next four centuries, Botticelli's incomplete but transcendentally lovely illustrations disappeared, until they were rediscovered and purchased for the German government in 1882 by Friedrich Lippmann, the art historian and curator of Berlin's Kupferstichkabinett, a museum of prints and drawings.

FIGURE 7. Botticelli, *Map of Hell*, c. 1495. From Art Resource.

Today, ninety-two sheets of the planned illustrations are extant, with eighty-five held by Berlin's Kupferstichkabinett and seven in Rome's Vatican Library, which also holds the masterpiece of the project, Botticelli's *Map of Hell* (Figure 7).

The *Map of Hell* is a remarkably detailed work that may be the single most powerful visual interpretation of Dante ever produced. Botticelli was just one of many Renaissance authors to "map" Dante's afterworld, a tradition that had begun with the brilliant charts and guides to Inferno created by Antonio Manetti, a contemporary of Botticelli's and author of a biography of Brunelleschi as well as *La novella del grasso legnaiuolo* (The story of the fat woodworker), a humorous tale of switched identity that illuminates the age's obsession with perspective. This desire for a "topographical" Dante was inspired by the broader Renaissance trend of rationalizing pictorial space and making canvases look three-dimensional, a process that stretched back to Brunelleschi's experiment with one-point perspective and that was eventually codified by Leon Battista Alberti in *De pictura* (On painting, 1435).[9] Breaking with the more flat, two-dimensional images of medieval art, Renaissance painters sought to create the illusion of realistic space and perfectly receding vanishing points in works like Leonardo's *Last Supper* (1495–98) and Raphael's *School of Athens* (1517), among countless others.

The remarkable level of detail in the *Map of Hell* shows that, in terms of artistic precision, Botticelli went further than any previous Dantesque cartographer, including Manetti. It also suggests the depth of Botticelli's intellectual engagement with Dante. The Florentine painter, who had never formally studied literature and who had been accused by his biographer Giorgio Vasari of having "wasted his time" in illustrating Dante, submitted Dante's afterworld to the cool, rational skepticism of his humanist mind.[10] Dante's punishments are all there in Botticelli's *Map*, represented in painstaking clarity. But because of the order and balance of his images, the fire and brimstone of Inferno feels muted, its dark energies absorbed by the pristine logic of the Florentine artist's attention to detail and expert rendering of space.

As a piece of literary criticism, Botticelli's illustrations of *Inferno* do a superb job of conveying Dante's system of sin and punishment. But their bird's-eye perspective may make them less convincing as "close readings." They often fail to bring out the complex psychologies of sinners whose neurosis and astonishing capacity for self-deception have mesmerized readers for centuries. Nowhere is that gap in Infernal portraiture more jarring than in Botticelli's rendering of *Inferno* 26 (Figure 8), the celebrated canto of Ulysses, the ancient Greek hero whose enchanting,

FIGURE 8. Botticelli, *Inferno* 26. From Art Resource.

seductive words as a "false counselor" lead his men to death at sea, after they succumb to an eloquence that would inspire, as we will see, later writers ranging from Mary Shelley to Primo Levi. In Botticelli's illustration, Ulysses and his companion, the fierce Diomedes, merely appear as fleeting profiles sandwiched in between the waves of flame that cover the parchment, their personalities swept away by the tidal force of Botticelli's line.

But what Botticelli sacrificed in detail he more than made up for in structure. His mastery of what Giorgio Vasari called *disegno*—the capacity for "drawing" or "design" that in his view elevated Florentine artists above all other contemporaries, especially the more color-focused Venetians—enabled Botticelli to use drawing as a cognitive tool that revealed the essence of *Inferno* in flickering silverpoint. By rendering Inferno with such clarity, Botticelli blended Dante's medieval ethos with the more scientifically inclined protocols of the Renaissance.

Despite the glories of Botticelli's *Inferno* illustrations, especially the *Map of Hell*, it is in *Purgatorio* where the particular nature or visual poetics of his interpretation of Dante becomes manifest. The transition from the drama of *Inferno* to the more subdued world of *Purgatorio* may be one of the most jolting, and one of the most perfectly executed, in Western literature. The bottom of Dante's hell is so removed from the warmth of God's love that it is covered in ice, ruled over by a three-headed Satan who devours history's greatest villains in his grinding maw. Then, suddenly, after the magical closing lines of *Inferno*—"then we came forth to see again the stars" (*e quindi uscimmo a riveder le stelle, Inf.* 34.139),[11] Dante the pilgrim and Virgil the guide find themselves in a realm as sweet as its predecessor was bitter:

> The gentle hue of oriental sapphire
> in which the sky's serenity was steeped—
> its aspect pure as far as the horizon—
> brought back my joy in seeing just as soon
> as I had left behind the air of death
> that had afflicted both my sight and breast.

> *Dolce color d'orïental zaffiro,*
> *che s'accoglieva nel sereno aspetto*
> *del mezzo, puro infino al primo giro,*
> *a li occhi miei ricominciò diletto,*
> *tosto ch'io usci' fuor de l'aura morta*
> *che m'avea contristati li occhi e 'l petto.* (*Purg.* 1.13–18)

No translation, no matter how expert, can capture the dizzying transition from Dante's dense, visceral language in *Inferno* 34, with its cannibalistic Satan, to the light and airy atmosphere of Mount Purgatory and its promise of hard-won redemption. A line like "dolce color d'oriental zaffiro" (the gentle hue of oriental sapphire) does more than establish a lexical break with hell's brutal rhetoric: it also restores the spirits of Dante's readers.

Botticelli managed to visualize this shift right from the start of the new canticle (Figures 9 and 10): Mount Purgatory appears in the distance, expertly detailed to a greater degree than ever before,[12] and it is fronted by a cinematic sequence in which Dante and the sinners arrive on the shores and receive instructions from gatekeeper Cato on how to expiate their sins. The setting is as calm, sparse, and serene as the language it represents. Gone is hell's busy, energetic swirl and crowded geography. For the first time in Botticelli's cycle, the human figure begins to emerge, no longer swallowed up by its topographical coordinates.

Human time resurfaces in Purgatorio after the static temporal realm of Inferno, where sinners exist in an eternal now, nailed forever to the cross of sins that they repeat in a vicious feedback loop by recounting them to the passing pilgrim, Dante.[13] Meanwhile, in Purgatorio, hell's immobile sinners give way to restless penitents, who climb toward heaven in steps measured in days, years, and centuries. Saving your soul requires patience: it took the father of humankind, Adam, some 5,232 years to make it to Paradiso, after 930 years of sinful life on earth and then another 4,302 in Limbo, where, like the others in that realm, he abided "in desire without hope" (sanza speme ... in disio, Inf. 4.42). Botticelli understood that this new temporal dimension of Dante's universe compelled him to switch from mapping Dante's landscapes, which had been his practice in illustrating Inferno, to

FIGURES 9 AND 10. Botticelli, *Purgatorio* 1 (top) and 2 (bottom).
From Art Resource.

focusing on the slow, winding path to redemption of his penitential characters.

His illustration of *Purgatorio* 2 exemplifies this more human-centered approach. Here Dante meets the shade of Casella, a former friend and medieval performer who set to music and sang the verses of writers including Dante. In *Purgatorio*, he launches into a rendition of one of the Sweet New Style poems that Dante composed while under the sway of Guido Cavalcanti:

> "Love that discourses to me in my mind"
> [Casella] then began to sing—and sang so sweetly
> that I still hear that sweetness sound in me.

> *"Amor che ne la mente mi ragiona"*
> *cominciò elli allor sì dolcemente,*
> *che la dolcezza ancor dentro mi suona.* (112–14)

The release of these dulcet words, with their aching variations on *dolcezza*/sweetness, causes the otherwise dutiful penitents, Dante among them, to stop dead in their tracks and listen—until stern Cato arrives to break up the impromptu gathering and hustle the shades onward, haranguing them as "laggard spirits" (*spiriti lenti*, *Purg.* 2.120). Botticelli captures the tenderness of the encounter by featuring the failed embrace between Dante and the bodyless form of his long-lost companion (as we learn repeatedly in *Purgatorio*, you cannot "treat a shade as a solid thing").[14] He also depicts the relentless forward movement of the penitents, urged on by Cato's rebuke. Time returns to *Purgatorio*, and with it comes motion. Botticelli registers that change by concentrating his stylus on itinerant souls intent on bridging the distance between sin and salvation.

The left half of the drawing for *Purgatorio* 10, the canto where Dante learns humility by seeing it represented in beautifully

FIGURE 11. Botticelli, *Purgatorio* 10. From Art Resource.

sculpted forms, is typically sparse and delicate (Figure 11). But the right part of the leaf, which features the pagan Roman emperor Trajan showing kindness to a poor woman, shows an uncharacteristically busy, crowded scene that recalls Botticelli's *Inferno*. It also brings us inside what art historian Michael Baxandall called the "period eye," how people from a given era process and represent visual experience.[15] The military scene refers to one of the better-known works of the era, Paolo Uccello's *Battle of San Romano* (Figure 12), a set of three paintings on a decisive encounter between Florentine and Sienese forces in 1432, which Botticelli reimagines by applying the new laws of mathematical perspective that give the illustration its architectonic feel. The leaf thus infuses the more free-form and abstract qualities of Botticelli's *Purgatorio* drawings with a strong dose of

FIGURE 12. Paolo Uccello, *The Counterattack of Micheletto da Cotingola at the Battle of San Romano*, c. 1455 (from *The Battle of San Romano*). From Art Resource.

the *disegno* that enabled him to map Dante's hell with such accuracy.

The painter's well-publicized love of a good prank surprisingly resurfaces in the illustration.[16] Beneath the kneeling, humble Trajan on the far left—a sign that Christian virtue can miraculously affect even a pagan—two stones come spontaneously to life and start walking on human feet, an allegory for the canto's larger theme of how art can seem lifelike. This visual wink suggests how the *Commedia* continued to inspire the popular, less rarefied imaginations of the Renaissance.

Botticelli depicts Beatrice in *Purgatorio* 30 as resplendent in her chariot while an overwhelmed Dante kneels before her. She presides over a divine procession that matches the *Map of Hell* in level of detail, as its portrayals include twenty-four elders holding aloft the books of the Hebrew Bible, a griffin that represents the mix of divinity and humanity in Christ, and seven heavenly servants who strew Beatrice's path with roses and lilies. It is no wonder that a leading Botticelli scholar, the connoisseur Bernard Berenson, found the scene so moving.[17] Its illustration of the long-awaited reunion between the pilgrim and his muse sets in motion what many consider the most successful element in all of Botticelli's cycle: his focus on the dynamic relation between Dante and Beatrice. Botticelli's legendary biographer, Herbert Horne, was as enraptured as Berenson, writing that the painter's illustrations of this Earthly Paradise "stand out from the rest of [his] drawings by reason of the sumptuous beauty of their design," as the outward elements of the drawings "become expressive of the spirit and of things spiritual" in a unique way for this otherwise earthy painter.[18]

"The only simplicity to be trusted is the simplicity to be found on the far side of complexity," the philosopher Alfred North Whitehead once remarked, a notion that applies to Dante's *Paradiso* and Botticelli's version of it.[19] Early on, Dante alerts the reader to the challenge of what will be his most demanding canticle:

> O you who are within your little bark,
> eager to listen, following behind
> my ship that, singing, crosses to deep seas,
> turn back to see your shores again: do not
> attempt to sail the seas I sail; you may,
> by losing sight of me, be left astray.
> The waves I take were never sailed before.

> *O voi che siete in piccioletta barca,*
> *desiderosi d'ascoltar, seguiti*
> *dietro al mio legno che cantando varca,*
> *tornate a riveder li vostri liti:*

non vi mettete in pelago, ché forse,
perdendo me, rimarreste smarriti. (*Purg.* 2.1–6)

The linguistic inventiveness of Dante's *Paradiso* reflects the terra incognita of the last leg of his journey, a realm beyond mortal comprehension. A cascade of neologisms fills *Paradiso*, most of them simple words recast into new forms by prefixes and suffixes, including "to enthree oneself" (*intrearsi*), "to engod oneself" (*indiarsi*), and "to eternalize itself" (*insemprarsi*).[20] Fittingly, Dante encapsulates the verbal challenges presented by these ineffable states in *Paradiso* 1 with an invented word: "To transhumanize cannot be put in words" (*Trasumanar significar* per verba / *non si poria*, 70–71).[21]

Reading such a line, Botticelli likely wondered what it meant for him to try and cast this ineffable language into images. A lasting impression inspired by his drawings of *Paradiso* is the power of subtraction. To a greater degree than in *Purgatorio*, his choice of subject matter in *Paradiso* feels pointed and selective: he repeatedly employs just a few spare visual tropes, often set against empty backgrounds. Perhaps the painter was simply rushed and running out of time as he worked his way through the final canticle. According to one plausible theory, Botticelli may have been forced to abandon the Dante project and finish it up as best he could if his patron Lorenzo di Pierfrancesco had in fact demanded it as a gift for the French royal court around 1494–95.[22] Regardless of the circumstances, Botticelli hit his stride in illustrating *Paradiso*, arriving at that intensely personal reading of Dante and level of pictorial abstraction celebrated by Berenson, among others.[23] Botticelli's shift from the realism of his *Inferno* to the more ethereal and approximate drawings of *Paradiso* followed Dante's own model: at one point, Beatrice explains to Dante that what he is seeing is not heaven's "reality,"

FIGURE 13. Botticelli, *Paradiso* 10. From Art Resource.

which is beyond his human faculties, but rather a heavenly expression of light that "condescends / to human powers."[24]

One could say as much of Botticelli's illustrations. Heaven becomes the site for the private story of Dante and Beatrice, their movements unimpeded by the other blessed souls who populate the realm. In Botticelli's rendering of the sequence on saints Francis and Dominic from *Paradiso* 11 to 12, we see only Dante and Beatrice with no trace of those august theologians. Yet the force and logic of Botticelli's Dante-Beatrice motif become evident when one contemplates them in sequence and in the aggregate. The soft, whirring energy of Beatrice and Dante's joyous flight through the poem's final spheres is palpable, as are the subtle exchanges between the two figures and their changing expressions and body movements, as we see in canto 10 (Figure 13).

In a major departure from Dante, Botticelli gave actual bodies to the poet's more ethereal figures of light in *Paradiso*. He even affixed his signature to his illustration of canto 28, the only drawing ever signed by the painter. The gesture is fitting: the human body, with its capacity for gestural expressivity in paintings like his renowned *The Birth of Venus* and *Primavera*, was arguably Botticelli's primary "signature," the surest way to identify a work as his and his alone.[25] That "embodied" signature is everywhere in his illustration of *Paradiso* 28, as he renders Dante's hosts of angels as *corposi*, full-bodied, Renaissance putti with radiant faces, rounded limbs, and bouncing curls.

Botticelli's project suggests the popularity of Dante among the creative minds of his hometown during the Renaissance. Part of the reason lay in Dante's Florentine roots. Landino's landmark edited volume of 1481, the first printed text of the *Commedia* to appear in the city, was symptomatic of the poet's cult-like celebrity status in Florence. Soon after Dante's death in 1321 and culminating in Boccaccio's public lectures on Dante at Santo Stefano in Badia in 1373–74, the poet's work was celebrated by the city that had banished him. The *Commedia* was memorized by local workers, taught in schools, and considered a sacred civic text, as we see in Domenico di Michelino's painting from 1465 (Figure 14), which appeared just before Landino's volume and Botticelli's illustrations.

Dante's surging posthumous reputation in Renaissance Florence, however, did not come without its pitfalls. As we have seen, many highbrow and religiously conservative thinkers rejected it as either inelegant or dangerously heretical. Evidence of the dichotomous fate of the *Commedia* surfaced in two related phenomena, one punctuated and self-contained, the other of long duration. The first, which occurred in 1555, changed the way we read Dante forever. The original title of his work, the

FIGURE 14. Domenico di Michelino, *Dante Holding the "Divine Comedy" in Florence*, 1465. From Art Resource.

Comedìa, was purposefully humble: unlike lofty epic predecessors, Dante's *poema sacro* would blend high and low languages and literary styles to give the full range of the Tuscan vernacular. It was "comic" not in the humorous sense—one would be hard-pressed to find a less funny work in the history of literature—but in the Aristotelian sense. As the Greek philosopher theorized, comedy distinguished itself from tragedy by treating low subject matter, in this case the Florentine citizen-exile, Dante Alighieri, who was no prince or "personage of great estate" as a later definition of tragedy from Shakespeare's time would describe the term.[26] One should note how this notion of comedy has migrated through literary history to mean, essentially, a tale that ends well, as the *Commedia* certainly does, with its pilgrim approaching his Christian God and attaining his own salvation. In secular terms, this literary-historical notion of the "happy ending" is perhaps best exemplified by Shakespeare's comedies and their tendency to end at the marriage altar, thus ensuring a joyful narrative closure and a strengthening of social codes through the institution of lawful matrimony.

But in 1555 a Venetian printer named Gabriele Giolito de' Ferrari changed once and for all the claims to humility inscribed in Dante's original title. He inserted the word *Divina* (*divine*) before the modernized Italian spelling *Commedia* in a beautiful edition of the poem edited by the eminent Venetian belletrist Lodovico Dolce. From that day forward, the work was, by implication, inspired by heaven itself. In truth, the genealogy for the appellation *divino* for Dante's work stretched all the way back to Boccaccio and his myth-filled *Little Treatise in Praise of Dante*, which claimed that God had sent Dante to the Florentines and all Italians to renew literature. With the word *divine* now stamped forever on the title page of the *Commedia*, Giolito's typographical verdict added to the aura of Dante's already burnished legend. As a publisher, Giolito was keen on attracting as broad a reading public as possible, so he actively promoted vernacular authors like Dante, Petrarch, and Boccaccio in annotated volumes that made these difficult authors accessible to less experienced readers.[27] Giolito became successful in the competitive world of Renaissance publishing, second in importance only to the Venetian powerhouse Aldine.[28] It is safe to surmise that adding the word *divina* to the title of Dante's epic both affirmed his special place in the vernacular canon and boosted Giolito's sales.

The second, decidedly less glorious indicator of Dante's Renaissance and post-Renaissance fate could be found in the publication statistics of this now "divine" *Comedy*. While new editions of the *Commedia* appeared with great frequency during the fifteenth and sixteenth centuries, in the seventeenth century things dramatically changed. Not a single edition of the *Commedia* was published in Europe between 1629 and 1702. In hindsight, we can see more clearly that these two centuries were the low point of Dante's afterlife. The causes for Dante's eclipse were as complicated as they were various—and, as we will see, they were held together by a few overriding assumptions that came to shadow the reception of the *Commedia* like a black cloud.

Chapter 4

The Lost Centuries

IN HIS STUDY of responses to Dante's *Commedia* over the centuries, Michael Caesar poignantly asks: "Why was Dante not popular in the seventeenth century?"[1] The factual basis for the question is undeniable: whereas twenty-nine editions of Dante's epic had appeared in the previous century, in the 1600s a scant three were published, all in the first three decades and all in northern Italy (Vicenza 1613, Padua 1629, Venice 1629).[2] Not even Dante's hometown of Florence, which by this time had transitioned from free-standing republic to Medici grand duchy, bothered to usher in a new edition. The reception desert engulfed Dante's other writings as well: of the minor works (the *opere minori*), only *De vulgari eloquentia* was published, in passing as it were, in an anthology devoted to books on proper elocution in 1643.

The *Commedia* was facing both formal and ideological headwinds. An author like Dante, who chose the pagan Virgil as his guide, was bound to receive his share of grief in Counter-Reformation circles. Though his *Commedia* was never placed in the Index of Forbidden Books, his *De monarchia* landed there in 1585 and would not be removed until 1881. Meanwhile, invectives against the *Commedia* from within the Church continued into the seventeenth century. Galileo's archrival, Cardinal Robert Bellarmine, highlighted unacceptable passages from Dante in his *Disputationes de controversiis Christianae fidei adversus hujus temporis haereticos* (Disputations on the controversies of the Christian faith against the heretics of this time, 1586–1593); the scholar Bellisario Bulgarini announced that there was "very little that was Christian" about the *Commedia* in 1616; and the poet and critic Tommaso Stagliani surmised that if Dante's poem were not so obscure, it would have drawn more ire from the Inquisition.[3]

Dante's decline in the 1600s had much to do with changing literary tastes. In what Caesar describes as the "hedonistic" world of Seicento aesthetics, Dante's sobriety, moralism, and arch-seriousness fell flat. Baroque or "broken pearl" aesthetics valued excess, ornamentation, and rhetorical flair—a program of art-for-art's-sake that was nowhere to be found in a poem where Paolo and Francesca suffer damnation for an adultery sparked by reading "for pleasure" (*per diletto, Inf.* 5.127). By the seventeenth century, Dante was no longer considered the literary maverick that he had been hailed as throughout the Renaissance. As Caesar writes, in this age of "wingèd chariots" and other literary extravagances, the humble vernacular of Dante, once so revolutionary, did not stand a chance.[4]

Dante's decline in appeal throughout the seventeenth century was incontrovertible—but there were notable exceptions. For one thing, the gradual consolidation of Dante scholarship, which had gathered momentum in the Renaissance in the robust commentary tradition, continued apace in the seventeenth century.[5] The massive attention devoted to individual lines in the *Commedia* made it akin to the traditions of biblical commentary. The scholar Benedetto Buonmattei, secretary of Florence's prestigious Accademia della Crusca, a safeguard of Tuscan linguistic purity, gave a staggering number of 466 lectures on the *Comme-dia* between 1632 and 1657. But not a single official commentary appeared in the seventeenth century. In fact, the period between Lodovico Castelvetro's commentary in 1572 and that of Pompeo Venturi in 1732 represents the longest lacuna, by far, in this hallowed category of Dante's reception. But this dramatic gap did not necessarily mean that scholarly inquiry into the *Commedia* flagged in the 1600s. Buonmattei was hardly alone among his contemporaries in exploring the mysteries and forms of what was by then considered Dante's canonical epic.

A second key aspect of seventeenth-century responses to Dante—again, one already present in the Renaissance—was Dante's status as iconoclast: in the words of the prophet-philosopher Tommaso Campanella from 1596, Dante rose above the "common rules," thereby revealing the "divine spirit of [this] architectonic poet."[6] While Dante's irrepressible individuality and resistance to categorization garnered the hostility of more classically minded literati, whom Campanella derided as "fatuous grammarians," many others found refuge and inspiration in Dante's sui generis talents.[7] The question of where Dante did and did not fit in the age's rules-based system of literary composition transcended the cozy confines of elite Italian literary culture. One need only recall the divided early responses to another literary genius who flouted rhetorical prescriptions, Shakespeare, to imagine how divisive Dante's unique aesthetics could be. His lack of adherence to rules was an especially sore point during the rise of literary neoclassicism in the Enlightenment, another lost century for the *Commedia*. Thus it was hardly surprising that Voltaire, the eighteenth-century author who spent the most energy in attacking Dante—he once referred to the *Commedia* as a "monster" (*mostre*)—also called the rule-breaking Shakespeare a "drunken savage."[8]

During the 1600s and 1700s, Dante was no longer thought to be the golden child of Italian letters as he had been in the first flush of his fame, which had begun while he was still alive and extended into the Renaissance. Nor had he yet become the global force in literature that would result from his rise to übercanonical status in the Romantic age and beyond, all the way to the present. Despite this critical resistance to Dante, the seventeenth and eighteenth centuries actually represent one of the most fascinating chapters in the reception of the *Commedia* because of the unexpected reversals they produced. What had previously been considered virtues in Dante—his originality, iconoclasm, and visionary force—suddenly became liabilities. And what had once been thought of as a Dantesque deficit, especially his occasional uncouthness and persistent rawness, could become praiseworthy.[9]

The towering figure of the English poet John Milton and his reading of Dante straddle that divide between, on the one hand, an awareness of Dante's untimeliness and eccentricity and, on the other, the realization that even in his unpopularity Dante held special powers for any author wise and contrarian enough to discern them. Like Dante, Milton was both of his age yet apart from it. He saw things in the power of literature—and Dante's writing—that other contemporary writers lacked the vision to access. So rather than being an index of Dante's status in seventeenth-century Europe, Milton was a beacon of its possibilities. The connection between England's and Italy's greatest epic poets was natural and deep.[10] Milton had thrilled to the Italian language since childhood: his best friend was the Italian-born Charles Diodati, a classmate at London's St. Paul's Grammar School, and he authored six poems in Italian. His virtuoso understanding of the Petrarchan sonnet form is evident in masterpieces like his poem on his blindness, "When I consider how my light is spent" (c. 1652–55).[11] Milton once called Italy "the home of humane studies and of all civilized teaching,"[12] and he spent a formative two-month period in Florence in 1639, when he was in this thirties. He imbibed the commemorative atmosphere surrounding the city's exiled hero Dante, while also visiting with such living legends as the aged Galileo, who was recovering from years of interrogation and had become completely blind. Throughout his career, Milton referred not only to the *Commedia* but also to Dante's less-known *De monarchia* and *Convivio*. The polyglot Milton was also familiar with Dante's *De vulgari eloquentia* as well as his Latin epistles. And he referenced Boccaccio's *Little Treatise in Praise of Dante*, which was published in the same volume as the original printed copy of Dante's *Vita nuova* in 1576. This book was part of Milton's personal library, suggesting an intimate acquaintance.[13]

In addition to the bold affinities between Milton and Dante, there were also stark differences between *Paradise Lost* and the *Commedia*: Dante's Satan is as empty and vacuous as Milton's is complex and beguiling; Dante's Adam and Eve spend just several hours in an Eden that feels, by contrast, fully and extensively inhabited by Milton's primeval couple; and Dante's intensely doctrinal, abstract representation of heaven as a divine light show is a world apart from Milton's warring angels and stirring scenes of battle in the celestial spheres. An odd but telling document from the eighteenth century, Mark Akenside's "Ballance of the Poets" from 1746—a ranking of literary greats from Homer and Virgil to Ariosto and Pope—gives a sense of how varied Dante and Milton were in their approaches to literary composition. In "Dramatic Expression," Dante scores only 8 out of 20, while the more narrative-driven Milton clocks in with a respectable 15, and in "Taste," the occasionally crude Dante scores 8 compared to the classicizing Milton's robust 18.[14]

While we should take such naïve metrics with a grain of salt, the discrepancies between the two poets' styles are clearly reflected in the numbers, which, as expected, set Dante on the lower end in this period of his languishing popularity.

Yet when we look beneath the surfaces of Dante's and Milton's epics, we find much common ground on key issues.[15] One shared principle, in particular, was essential to both the *Commedia* and *Paradise Lost*—one could even call it their spiritual DNA. Dante makes clear that, of all the gifts from God to humankind, one stands out: free will. The primacy of moral agency is articulated in *Purgatorio* 16, when Marco Lombardo underscores that there would be no point in creating a hell of woe or a heaven of bliss if we as human agents did not have "free will" (*libero arbitrio*, 71). The freedom to choose in a world created by an omnipotent, all-knowing god leads to a fundamental paradox of Christianity—one acknowledged and embraced by Dante as well as Milton.[16] Both believed that though God knows all that will occur to humankind through the laws of divine Providence, humans still have the right, indeed the necessity, to make moral choices in freedom. As Beatrice notes to Dante in *Paradiso* 5:

> "The greatest gift the magnanimity
> of God, as He created, gave, the gift
> most suited to His goodness, gift that He
> most prizes, was the freedom of the will;
> those beings that have intellect—all these
> and none but these—received and do receive
> this gift."

> "*Lo maggior don che Dio per sua larghezza*
> *fesse creando, e a la sua bontate*
> *più conformato, e quel ch'e' più apprezza,*
> *fu de la volontà la libertate;*

di che le creature intelligenti,
e tutte e sole, fuoro e son dotate." (19–24)

This notion of free will as the "greatest gift" (*maggior don*) is anticipated toward the end of *Purgatorio*, in Virgil's valedictory words:

"Await no further word or sign from me:
your will is free, erect, and whole—to act
against that will would be to err: therefore
I crown and miter you over yourself."

"Non aspettar mio dir più né mio cenno;
libero, dritto e sano è tuo arbitrio,
e fallo fora non fare a suo senno:
per ch'io te sovra te corono e mitrio." (*Purg.* 27.139–42)

In what we might call the "graduation scene" of Dante the pilgrim, Virgil indicates that his protégé is ready to go forth because he has completed an intellectual, moral, and ethical tutelage that finds his will upright and sound. He is now free to enter heaven.

Without directly referencing Dante's writings, Milton reserves a similarly exalted place for free will. In book 3, it surges to the fore in the Argument, which finds God sitting on his throne alongside Jesus, while Satan flies toward the newly created world, ready to wreak havoc on Adam and Eve. God tells Jesus the sad tale that is about to transpire in Eden, yet crucially he also "clears His own justice and wisdom from all imputation," describing how he "created Man free and able enough to have withstood his tempter."[17] As God explains, the issue comes down to free will and its relation to justice. Without the consequences of moral choice, "Grace cannot be extended towards Man." Book 3 puts the matter explicitly:

"For man will hearken to [Satan's] glozing lies
And easily transgress the sole command,
Sole pledge of his obedience. So will fall
He and his faithless progeny. Whose fault?
Whose but his own? Ingrate! He had of Me
All he could have. I made him just and right,
Sufficient to have stood though free to fall." (93–99)

Milton's God goes on to say that freedom of the will imbues humankind with a force equal to the divine. As God's words reveal, his foreknowledge of Adam and Eve's fall does not in any way impact their independence of choice—and personal responsibility—in engineering their own demise:

. . . "They therefore, as to right belonged,
So were created, nor can justly accuse
Their Maker or their making or their fate,
As if predestination overruled
Their will disposed by absolute decree
Or high foreknowledge. They themselves decreed
Their own revolt, not I. If I foreknew
Foreknowledge had no influence on their fault
Which had no less proved certain unforeknown." (111–19)

Summing up this majestic gift of free will that is soon to be abused in Eden, God continues: "They trespass, authors to themselves in all / Both what they judge and what they choose, for so / I formed them free and free they must remain" (122–24).

The discourse on free will reaches its dramatic pitch in book 4 in the confrontation on the battlefields of heaven, when Satan furiously cries to his rival, the archangel Gabriel:

"Hadst thou the same free will and pow'r to stand?
Thou hadst. Whom hast thou then or what t' accuse

But Heav'n's free love dealt equally to all?
Be then His love accursed, since love or hate
To me alike it deals eternal woe!
Nay cursed be thou since against His thy will
Chose freely what it now so justly rues.
Me miserable!" (66–73)

The repetition of the word *will* in the space of just a few lines
underscores Satan's visceral understanding of the path that he
has freely chosen as well as his willingness to risk eternal bondage and suffering in order to pursue his own agenda. The circu-
larity of his words and their convoluted logic serve as a brilliant
rhetorical reminder of how Satan's twisted reasoning corrupts
the understanding of free will that had been laid out so clearly
by God to Jesus just a book earlier.

Milton's notion of free will cannot be said to come wholly or
even directly from Dante. In preparing his poem, he studied
other influential works, including Erasmus's celebration of free
will in *De libero arbitrio* (On free will, 1524) and Martin Luther's
more pessimistic refutation of Erasmus's position in *De servo
arbitrio* (On the bondage of the will, 1525). In this seminal
Renaissance theological debate, Erasmus argued that all
humans possessed free will and that the preemptive doctrine of
predestination went against the teachings of the Bible. Luther
countered by proposing that original sin impeded humans from
being able to bring about their own salvation and that there
could be no free will among humans overwhelmed by their
own inherently sinful nature.[18] As important as this exchange
between Erasmus and Luther had been for Milton, he also likely
noticed Dante's legendary treatment of free will, especially
because of his great love of Italian literature. And as a lifelong
reader of Dante's work, Milton almost certainly would have

pondered the Dantesque notion of free will as God's chief gift to humankind.

There is also a less grand, more intimate element to Milton's reading of Dante that complements the epic tenor of their common interest in free will. Earlier in his career, and while he still had his faculties of vision, the thirty-eight-year-old Milton—just past that Dantesque midpoint of life set at thirty-five in *The Divine Comedy*—wrote *Apology for Smectymnuus* (1642). One of his fierce pamphlets criticizing the Church of England, the tract argues that because defending the truth exposes one to personal attacks, the issue of individual integrity is paramount. After reviewing his own literary tastes and predilections, Milton wrote that even when he enjoyed an author's work, if the content was immoral or perverse, "their art I still applauded, but the men I deplored."[19] To his mind, two writers stood out above all for their "sublime and pure thoughts, without transgression": the "two famous renowners of Beatrice and Laura," respectively, Dante and Petrarch.[20] Milton concluded his homage to these founders of Italian literature with memorable words that certainly would have pleased the intensely autobiographical Dante: "he who would not be frustrate of his hope to write well hereafter in laudable things, ought himself to be a true poem; that is, a composition and pattern of the best and honourablest things; not presuming to sing high praises of heroic men, or famous cities, unless he have in himself the experience and the practice of all that which is praiseworthy."[21] In becoming "a true poem" himself, Milton drew on the literary energies of the *Commedia*.

———

Among the relatively few champions of the *Commedia* in the seventeenth and eighteenth centuries, an Italian figure on par with Milton emerged to promote Dante's cause: Giambattista Vico. Unlike Milton, whose fame took seed while he was alive and has spread ever since, Vico was a latecomer to intellectual celebrity. A relatively obscure academic, he taught rhetoric at the University of Naples and never managed to attain the more prestigious Chair of Jurisprudence that he coveted.[22] The marginality of Vico's career extended to his way of thinking: he was one of history's great "untimely" thinkers in the tradition of Friedrich Nietzsche and Jean-Jacques Rousseau. An eternal outsider, he ended his third-person autobiography, *Vita di Giambattista Vico* (Life of Giambattista Vico, c. 1725–32), with the defiant words that he "blessed all these adversaries as many occasions for withdrawing to his desk, as to his high impregnable citadel, to meditate and to write further works which he was wont to call 'so many noble acts of vengeance against his detractors.'"[23]

Vico's contrarian spirit, which the equally contentious Dante probably would have admired, found its most forceful distillation in his lifelong critique of René Descartes and his analytical model of thinking, which had come to dominate much of European philosophy. Vico criticized the Cartesian privileging of one's own mind as the filter and organizing principle of all knowledge, distilled in his famous dictum, *Cogito, ergo sum*: I think, therefore I am.[24] Vico countered that the highest form of truth could not be arrived at through observation or deduction but rather through invention or creation: we as humans, he argued, only know that which we have made, an axiom he expressed in the Latin phrase *verum esse ipsum factum*, truth is itself something made.[25]

Dante became central to this line of Vichian thinking, which would be elaborated and systematized in his magnum opus, *La scienza nuova* (The new science, 1744), the posthumously published work that eventually brought Vico the acclaim he lacked in his lifetime. For Vico, Dante was a "barbarous" thinker, the ultimate accolade from the Neapolitan philosopher, for he believed that it was among those early original and visionary thinkers that the future was made. Vico celebrated Dante's Middle Ages, as he did Homer's ancient Greece, as times of powerful imagination and larger-than-life figures, a far cultural cry from more modern and rational periods—Cartesian epochs par excellence—that represented what Vico contemptuously called "the barbarism of reflection."[26]

Surprisingly, Dante does not figure much in *The New Science*, though Vico does refer to him in passing as "the Tuscan Homer."[27] The allusion is significant: a key part of *The New Science* is book 3, "The Discovery of the True Homer," which uses philological tools to claim not only that the *Iliad* and the *Odyssey* were created by different authors but also that "Homer" himself was a purely invented construct. Instead, Vico argues, "the Greek peoples were themselves Homer," that is, the epics were not written by a single individual but rather compiled and orally transmitted over the generations by the peoples of ancient Greece.[28] The implications of this point extend far beyond philology and literary history: by making the early Greeks capable of the sublime poetry of Homeric epic, Vico was promoting the primal creative forces of early "poetic" cultures. For Vico, the term *poetry* meant far more than the composition of verse or the crafting of literary form; seizing on its etymology from the ancient Greek ποίησις, *poiesis*, "creative making," Vico believed that the inventive force of the poetic mode rendered it capable of uniting the diverse branches of knowledge in the arts and sciences.[29] To that end, his book 2 of *The New Science*, by far the longest of the work, is devoted to "Poetic Wisdom" and proposes that these imaginary and vital forms and cultural expressions of a people appear *before* the philosophical and rational developments that are in fact entirely derived from them.

Vico went on to write a philological note, "The Discovery of the True Dante," which he likely intended to send to the editor of a new commentary on Dante's *Commedia* by Pompeo Venturini in 1729. In it, Vico notes that Dante should be read on three counts: "as a history of the barbaric times in Italy, as the source of very beautiful Tuscan ways of speaking, and as an example of sublime poetry."[30] The note goes on to strengthen the parallels between Dante and Homer: according to Vico, each sang of his people at an early vibrant stage of cultural development; each collected the dialects and patterns of speech of his environs; and each achieved a sublime poetic register suitable to the robustness of his epoch (Vico contrasts this raw energy in Dante with what he calls the "delicate" verse of Petrarch and the "charming and graceful" prose of Boccaccio, two less powerful voices in his view).[31]

Vico continued to explore Dante's productive "barbarity" in a letter to his former pupil, the poet Gherardo degli Angioli. He began by reminding degli Angioli that he lived in a Cartesian age "made excessively lean by analytical methods" and overrun by a "philosophy which professes to deaden all those faculties of the soul that come to it from the body."[32] An antidote to this overly reflective age, Vico suggested, was degli Angioli's beloved Dante, "who seems rather too uncultured and coarse for the delicate fancies of today," a phrase that repeats that same word that Vico had negatively applied to Petrarch (*delicate*).[33] After diagnosing the speculative ills of the era, Vico explained why Dante, "born in the bosom of the wild and ferocious barbarism of Italy," was essential reading:

On account of such poverty of vernacular speech, Dante, in order to unfold his *Comedy*, had to assemble a language from those of all the peoples in Italy, in the same way that Homer had compiled his, using all those of Greece. Consequently, everyone recognizing their own native speech in his poems, all the Greek cities contested Homer to be their citizen. Thus Dante, furnished with poetic modes of speaking, employed his irascible genius in the *Comedy*.[34]

The message was clear: Vico's Dante was a new Homer, as both the Greek epics and the *Commedia* had been built up from the surging vernacular energies of their respective epochs. While Milton's Dantesque promotion of free will and Vico's creation of a "barbaric" Dante differ in terms of content, they share a devotion to the artistic power emanating from the *Commedia*. For Milton and Vico, Dante's poetic brilliance lay in his ability to reconceptualize the epic genre in a modern dialect that retained the luster of ancient cultural expression while reflecting the human emotions, religious needs, and intellectual dramas of the living present. All told, Milton and Vico not only "read" Dante; they imbibed his essence.

As the century progressed, especially in the Enlightenment, such visceral connections to Dante became exceedingly rare. Not only did the publication of Dante's work become less frequent, but many of the age's leading literary lights also did not bother to comment on Dante. Some began openly to attack him. Around the time Voltaire called Dante's epic a literary "hodge-podge," he delivered the unkindest cut of all: "Personne ne lit plus le Dante," he wrote in an edition of his *Philosophical Letters* from 1756: "Nobody reads Dante anymore." The remark is extraordinary, not in the literal sense because Dante remained one of the best-known writers from the Middle Ages, but because it reveals what little symbolic capital Dante's work had come to hold in elite circles. As usual, Voltaire was spot on: his fellow *philosophes* were even crueler than he. They did not attack the "crazy" Dante (*fou*, Voltaire's term of choice); they simply ignored him. Barely a line of Dante criticism or commentary can be found among the age's great thinkers, including the Dante agnostics Jean-Jacques Rousseau, Immanuel Kant, David Hume, Denis Diderot, and Jean le Rond d'Alembert, among many others.

There remained, however, areas of eighteenth-century culture where Dante's presence was still strong. An Italian expatriate in England, Giuseppe Baretti, wrote rapturously about Dante's "Beauties" in 1753, around the same time that Voltaire was skewering him. Early translations of the *Inferno* by the Frenchman Antoine Rivarol in 1785 and the English authors Charles Rogers in 1782 and Henry Boyd in 1785–1802 also appeared. But on the whole Dante's *Commedia* was out of sync with the Age of Light for a set of interrelated reasons. First, the poem was considered to be the embodiment of what many thinkers described as the Dark Ages, the medieval period that Edward Gibbon labeled a time of "barbarism and religion" and even derided as "rubbish."[35] Second, Dante's deeply religious work was viewed as unappealingly mystical and filled with doctrinal allegories that few Enlightenment *philosophes* were interested in tracing back to their biblical sources. And third, Dante's originality and experimentalism as an author—symptoms of that robust energy valued by Vico—were largely unappealing in the neoclassical, rule-bound literary culture of the Enlightenment, especially its French inflection.

This Enlightenment animus toward the *Commedia* culminated in an attack by a friend of Voltaire's, the Italian Jesuit Saverio Bettinelli.[36] Bettinelli's most scathing words against Dante appeared in his *Lettere virgiliane* (Virgilian letters, 1757), a text that describes a "reckless" modern versifier,[37] inspired by Dante, who has the bad judgment to extol Dante's work to a gathering of ancient poets, who, needless to say, are not impressed.[38] "The more one read" of Dante, Bettinelli writes, "the less one understood, even to each word there was a note, and to each note a commentary more obscure than the text." He goes on to quote Horace, saying that "poetry should impart both utility and pleasure." By contrast, Bettinelli posits, Dante's work only elicits uselessness and pain: it causes Lucretius to yawn, the Greeks to feel disgust, and Ovid to burst out laughing. The *Commedia* to Bettinelli was a mishmash of "sermons, dialogues, and questions, a poem without actions" and certainly not the work of a second Homer, as Vico had called him. The message was harsh and clear: "Dante was a great man despite the coarseness of his times and of his language," he writes. "But this does not mean that he should . . . be regarded as a classic author, when better ones have emerged."

That last assessment of Bettinelli's ("better ones have emerged") is perhaps more telling than his exaggerated critiques. On the whole, the seventeenth and eighteenth centuries were not happy ones for the *Commedia*. It continued to inspire brilliant interpretations and profound emotional responses. But it had also become fair game for the more intellectually conservative and self-consciously refined of literary minds. In 1684, John Dryden summed up Dante's fate during this transitional period:

> Dante's polished page
> Restored a silver, not a golden age.[39]

Chapter 5

Romantic Apotheosis

EVEN DANTE'S GREATEST champions would have had difficulty imagining the astonishing rebirth of interest in the *Commedia* after the Enlightenment and in the Romantic age. Dramatic historical events contributed to this change in fortune. Many young intellectuals, disillusioned with the French Revolution's descent into the bloody Reign of Terror and then the illiberal oppression of Napoleonic dictatorship, blamed these woes in part on the Enlightenment project's obsession with rational thought, anticlericalism, and human progress—the same criteria that had relegated Dante and his *Commedia* to second-class literary status. In the creative and cognitive realm of a post-revolutionary world, the new buzzwords were the *self*, *nature*, the *sublime*, and the *imagination*. The one writer whose work seemed to combine nearly all of those emerging cultural tropes was Dante.

Dante's writing turned up everywhere in Romantic Europe, from the pages of publishers to the daydreams of poets and the chatter in drawing rooms and coffee houses. Between 1800 and 1850, 181 editions of the *Comedy* were published in all corners of Europe, from Scotland and Spain to Russia and what today is Slovakia. Painters and illustrators were just as passionate as authors in their love of Dante: the *Commedia* was featured in the work of such celebrated Romantic artists as William Blake, Eugène Delacroix, Gustave Doré, and Francisco Goya, among many others. Stendhal summed up the Dante-mania in 1823: "the Romantic poet par excellence is Dante."[1] Readings of the *Commedia* during this time were not always accurate in a philological sense: some avid *dantisti* did not see him for what he was, an arch-Christian, but rather for what they wanted him to be—a secular literary hero for the ages. Much of the hero-mongering derived from the biographical sketches of Dante that appeared in many nineteenth-century editions of his work. One especially influential publication, Henry Francis Cary's translation of the *Commedia* in England, *The Vision* (1814), noted that Dante associated only with men of "grave and tragic deportment," an allusion to the poet's literary kinship with Milton.[2]

The topos of Dante as hero took flight in the Romantic era in ways that were often incongruous with the actual writing found in the *Commedia*. The English author and statesman Thomas Babington Macaulay, who like Cary believed in the intense symbiosis between Milton and Dante, offered an extreme version of this tendency. For Macaulay, Dante's life and poetry were one, as we see in these words of his from 1825:

> The Divine Comedy is a personal narrative. Dante is the eye-witness and ear-witness of that which he relates. . . . His own hands have grasped the shaggy sides of Lucifer. His own feet have climbed the mountains of expiation. . . . The reader would throw aside such a tale of incredible disgust, unless it were told with the strongest air of veracity, with a sobriety even in its horrors, with the greatest precision and multiplicity in its details.[3]

The athletic Dante evoked by Macaulay did not exist, nor does Dante's Christian epic translate into a "tale of incredible disgust."

Yet Macaulay's was just one of many overzealous Romantic interpretations to focus on the character "Dante" at the expense of his poetry. In truth, the Dantesque heroism so relished by the Romantics was of little importance in the *Commedia*, as Dante throughout the poem struggles to empty himself of pride and individuality. A principal theme of *Paradiso*, the canticle in which Dante encounters God, is "trasumanar," a neologism meaning "to transhumanize," to pass beyond the human (*Par.* 1.70)—and yet it was the proud and fierce Dantesque self that piqued Romantic interest.[4]

The trope of Dante the hero permeates what is arguably the quintessential Romantic novel: Germaine de Staël's *Corinne, ou Italie* (Corinne, or Italy, 1803). The daughter of Jacques Necker, Louis XVI's director of finance and a public hero in revolutionary France, Madame de Staël was always in the public eye and like Byron was known for her scandalous personal life, especially because of her long and stormy affair with the French author Benjamin Constant.[5] Her cultural interlocutors included Goethe, Gibbon, and Friedrich Schiller, and she had just as many powerful enemies as she did friends. One nemesis in particular proved especially dangerous: Napoleon loathed this free-thinking, free-speaking woman to such a degree that he had her exiled and had one of her books pulped. He was not alone in mocking Madame de Staël as "ugly," an insult that evokes the rampant misogyny directed at Madame de Staël by many in the male literary and political establishment. Her extravagant lifestyle and connection to the great thinkers of Romanticism coalesced in *Corinne*, a kind of creative manifesto of the entire Romantic age in which Dante features significantly.

Romantic tropes fill the novel, the story of a half-English, half-Italian poetess, Corinne, who falls in love with the brooding Scotsman Lord Nevil, who will eventually abandon the "unmarriageable" Corinne, whom Nevil considers too old (she is in her late twenties), too public as Italy's poet laureate, and too unconventional in her bohemian ways to be suitable for the altar. He marries instead Corinne's demure, virginal, and entirely conventional younger half-sister, the teenage English maiden Lucile. As a result, Corinne quite literally dies of a broken heart. It is not just the storyline that merits the tag "über-Romantic"; the book also openly explores now-obsolete issues like the vagaries of various national characters (the English are depicted as serious and honest, the Italians artistic and untrustworthy, the French charming and philosophical, and so on) and celebrates the sublime over the merely picturesque. And it luxuriates in the elemental force of nature and the deep connections between the living and the dead, two other Romantic tendencies.

In a key early scene, Corinne, dressed in the style of one of the Renaissance painter Domenichino's Sibyls, rides to the Capitoline Hill in a chariot and performs one of her famous improvisations to a large audience of admirers. Her song devotes three key stanzas to Dante:

> Now, if you love that glory which too oft
> Chooses its victims from its vanquishers,
> Those which itself has crown'd; think, and be proud
> Of days which saw the perish'd Arts reborn.
> Your Dante! Homer of the Christian age,
> The sacred poet of Faith's mysteries—
> Hero of thought—whose gloomy genius plunged
> In Styx, and pierced to hell; and whose deep soul
> Was like the abyss it fathom'd.[6]

In this first stanza, we find the Vichian motif of Dante as a new "Christian" Homer along with the pervasive Romantic image of Dante as a "gloomy genius," whose melancholic and independent worldview, in the manner of pre-Romantic predecessors like the eponymous suicidal protagonist of Goethe's *Die Leiden des jungen Werthers* (The sorrows of young Werther, 1774), transcends the mediocrity and corruption surrounding him. Madame de Staël also breaks with what had been previously considered in negative terms by anticlerical Enlightenment thinkers like Voltaire: for Corinne, Dante's immersion in "Faith's mysteries" is praiseworthy—though, ironically enough, the framework for her laudatory words on Dante are secular and not religious in any way. Most of the great Romantic readers of Dante were simply not interested in his Christian world. What drew them to the *Commedia* were Dante's worldly achievements, from his individual heroism to his magnificent poetic contributions to literary history. Corinne continues:

> Italia! as she was in days of power
> Revived in Dante: such a spirit stirr'd
> In old republics: bard and warrior too,
> He lit the fire of action 'mid the dead,
> Till e'en his shadows had more vigorous life
> Than real existence; still were they pursued
> By earthly memories; passions without aim
> Gnaw'd at their heart, still fever'd by the past;
> Yet less irrevocable seem'd that past,
> Than their eternal future.

The crux of this passage revolves around that unusual lexical coupling, "bard and warrior." Dante actually had been a warrior of sorts, having served as a cavalryman and endured hand-to-hand combat in the Battle of Campaldino of 1289 between his Guelphs and their rival Ghibellines. But Madame de Staël's Corinne is not concerned with Dante's soldierly career: she uses the term *warrior* in a more metaphysical sense, as one who waged cosmic cultural battles through poetry (hence the term *bard*, with its epic inflection) that "lit the fire of action 'mid the dead." The atmosphere of the passage is all Romantic fervor and fever, leaving us with the image of a Dante entirely consonant with the age's cult of the emotions. Corinne's improvisation continues in this same exalted key:

Methinks that Dante, banish'd from his own soil,
Bore to imagined worlds his actual grief,
Ever his shades inquire the things of life,
And ask'd the poet of his native land;
And from his exile did he paint a hell.
In his eyes Florence set her stamp on all;
The ancient dead seem'd Tuscans like himself:
Not that his power was bounded, but his strength;
And his great mind forced all the universe
Within the circle of its thought.

The heroism of Dante, Corinne's song makes clear, stems from his unmerited exile—the same note struck by her near contemporary, the Scottish philosopher Thomas Carlyle.[7] Madame de Staël's Dante has all the irruptive force of Vico's version of the poet and all the freedom of will of Milton's. But she goes a step further by personalizing Dante's struggles to such a degree that his poem becomes inseparable from his persona ("Not that his power was bounded, but his strength; / And his great mind forced all the universe / Within the circle of its thought"). With the Romantics, we come to a strange, often vexing paradox: the *Commedia* was now being printed and read throughout Europe with unprecedented frequency. Yet that "reading" was often predetermined or overdetermined by the age's obsession with the character of Dante himself, both as the heroic protagonist who struggles his way out of Inferno, through Purgatorio, and into Paradiso *and*, more generally, as the writer who beat all odds by writing a world-historical masterpiece from the depths of an unjust exile. In a visceral sense, and to the detriment of the actual religious content of the *Commedia*, the author had come to supplant his own text. With that Romantic occlusion, the Christian *Commedia* began to experience its secular apotheosis.

Crucially, Madame de Staël's heroine Corinne celebrates Dante from her perspective as an acclaimed poetess inhabiting a traditionally male public and creative sphere. She was not alone in this. Other female Romantics, including Anna Seward and Felicia Hemans, meditated on Dante's work as they considered issues of political and cultural identity and agency.[8] In the Victorian era that followed, Dante would also figure centrally in the work of such women writers as Claudia Hamilton Ramsay, Caroline Potter, Margaret Oliphant, Arabella Shore, and Mary MacGregor, all of whom labored to make Dante's work comprehensible to a wide readership.[9] As noteworthy as these other female authors were in their contribution to our understanding of Dante, another fellow nineteenth-century woman writer stands out even more, both for the brilliance of her work on Dante and for the long-standing resonance of her words.

Mary Shelley was, one could argue, born to interpret Dante. Her literary genes were almost unimaginably impeccable. Her mother was the visionary feminist author Mary Wollstonecraft, whose *Vindication of the Rights of Women* (1792) argued against male chauvinist authors like Rousseau by demanding that women be given the same education as men and not merely bred as sentimental appendages to their husbands and tasked with domestic chores. Meanwhile, her father was the leading free-thinking philosopher and political radical William Godwin. She would go on to marry the poet Percy Bysshe Shelley, one of the most brilliant readers of Dante ever—and one of the few capable of translating Dante's galloping *terza rima* into convincing English tercets. Mary and Percy read Dante together throughout their marriage, and the two of them lived in Italy for years, including lengthy stays in Dante's native Florence. As Diego Saglia has shown, Mary Shelley's engagement with Dante was not merely circumstantial: her representations of Dante embodied oppositional and liberal ideas of the nation in both "Giovanni Villani" (1823), her essay on the medieval Florentine chronicler, and *Valperga* (1823), her novel about the medieval Italian republics.[10]

Yet it is in her best-known work, the novel *Frankenstein* from 1818, that Shelley's insights into the *Commedia* are the most noteworthy. The story is familiar to many: an ambitious, talented scientist named Victor Frankenstein—in the original, he is the creator and not the created—fabricates a "monster" that he immediately disowns, repulsed by what he considers to be its gruesome ugliness. As a result, the creature begins a futile pursuit of the person whom he describes as his neglectful father and along the way commits a series of grisly murders, all of which he blames on Victor's refusal to acknowledge and care for him. Eventually, Frankenstein tries to hunt down the monster and destroy him before he can do any more harm, chasing him all the way to forlorn northern seas. Here is where we find him toward novel's end, as reported by Walton, the ship captain narrating this gothic tale. Victor has located the monster and is in hot pursuit, but the sailors do not want to continue, as the ship is lodged in dangerously icy waters. Victor then delivers a speech of stirring eloquence:

> "What do you mean? What do you demand of your captain? Are you, then, so easily turned from your design? Did you not call this a glorious expedition? And wherefore was it

glorious? Not because the way was smooth and placid as a southern sea, but because it was full of dangers and terror, because at every new incident your fortitude was to be called forth and your courage exhibited, because danger and death surrounded it, and these you were to brave and overcome. For this was it a glorious, for this was it an honourable undertaking. You were hereafter to be hailed as the benefactors of your species, your names adored as belonging to brave men who encountered death for honour and the benefit of mankind. . . . Oh! Be men, or be more than men. Be steady to your purposes and firm as a rock. This ice is not made of such stuff as your hearts may be; it is mutable and cannot withstand you if you say that it shall not. Do not return to your families with the stigma of disgrace marked on your brows. Return as heroes who have fought and conquered and who know not what it is to turn their backs on the foe."[11]

Readers of Dante may recognize the source of these words, translated or "carried over" by Shelley in the etymological sense of the term, into a new form that goes beyond mere citation and captures the burning spirit of Dante's original—thus following Dante's own prescription for strong reading.[12] I quote the passage at length to give the full sense of Victor's debt to the fatal eloquence of Ulysses in *Inferno* 26. Rightly considered one of the summits of Dante's poetic art, the canto's genius lies in its theatricality and originality. Homer's epic protagonist appears dramatically in the canto, as Virgil warns Dante not to try and speak directly to him and companion Diomedes: "since they were Greek, / perhaps they'd be disdainful of your speech" (*ch'ei sarebbero schivi, / perché fur greci, forse del tuo detto*, 74–75). When Ulysses does start speaking, there is no small talk: the hero launches into his life's story from inside his flame, buffeted by the wind and revving up like a powerful engine.[13] The canto boldly rewrites a source text that Dante only knew secondhand since he could not read Greek, yet which he succeeds in grasping profoundly. Dante's Ulysses is, ultimately, like Dante himself: a creature for whom exile is more than a political reality; it is a state of mind.

After leaving Circe, Dante's Ulysses discovers that more than any longing for home—the epic quality for which he has long been celebrated—an intellectual restlessness overtakes him, captured by Dante in these memorable lines:

> "neither my fondness for my son nor pity
> for my old father nor the love I owed
> Penelope, which would have gladdened her,
> was able to defeat in me the longing
> I had to gain experience of the world
> and of the vices and the worth of men."

> *"né dolcezza di figlio, né la pièta*
> *del vecchio padre, né 'l debito amore*
> *lo qual dovea Penelope far lieta,*
> *vincer potero dentro a me l'ardore*
> *ch'i' ebbi a divenir del mondo esperto,*
> *e de li vizi umani e del valore."* (94–99)

We might call this Ulysses' Faustian or "Frankenstein" moment: he yearns for total knowledge, at any price, even if it will cost him his soul (Faust) or the lives of his loved ones (Victor Frankenstein). Then Dante's Ulysses delivers the speech that caught Mary Shelley's ear:

> "Brothers," I said, "o you, who having crossed
> a hundred thousand dangers, reach the west,

...

Consider well the seed that gave you birth:
you were not made to live your lives as brutes,
but to be followers of worth and knowledge."

"O frati," dissi, "che per cento milia
perigli siete giunti a l'occidente,

...

Considerate la vostra semenza:
fatti non foste a viver come bruti,
ma per seguir virtute e conoscenza." (112–13, 118–20)

Shelley's inspiration could not be more evident: she too has Victor stand before his men and exhort them to greatness, as had Dante's Ulysses ("You were hereafter to be hailed as the benefactors of your species, your names adored as belonging to brave men who encountered death for honour and the benefit of mankind"). Like Dante's Ulysses, her Victor also underscores how past dangers have united the men for future glories common ("And wherefore was it glorious? Not because the way was smooth and placid as a southern sea, but because it was full of dangers and terror"). Again following Dante, her Victor reminds his men of their higher purpose in life, that they are not mere "brutes" but are made "to be followers of worth and knowledge" ("Do not return to your families with the stigma of disgrace marked on your brows. Return as heroes who have fought and conquered and who know not what it is to turn their backs on the foe").

Throughout her veiled allusion to Dante, Shelley riffs on a theme central to Dante's refashioning of the Homeric Ulysses: the consequences of pursuing knowledge without moral, ethical, or spiritual constraints. Remarkably, Shelley's channeling of Dante's source conveys the formidable ironies of Ulysses' speech. He *sounds* noble, but in truth he is manipulating his men into taking what Ulysses calls a "mad journey" (*folle volo*, *Inf.* 26.125) that will result in all their deaths. That is the reason, after all, that Ulysses suffers in hell as a false counselor enveloped in flame . Similarly, Victor Frankenstein, who throughout Shelley's text displays a narcissistic level of self-regard that prevents him from accepting the monster and preventing his multiple murders, is only trying to coerce the sailors to continue their journey because of his selfish desire to pursue the monster. Victor's honeyed eloquence ("Oh! Be men, or be more than men. Be steady to your purposes and firm as a rock. This ice is not made of such stuff as your hearts may be") is mere camouflage for his monomania.

Ultimately, both the canto of Ulysses and the novel *Frankenstein* are about impassable borders: in Dante, the Strait of Gibraltar crossed by Ulysses and his men represent the end of the known world and their passage into a terra incognita that is an allegory for Ulysses' boundless, unquenchable desire for knowledge. For Shelley, the icy landscapes where Victor follows the monster represent that mix of beauty and terror central to Romantic aesthetics as well as the fatal distance to which Victor will go in the hopes of exercising his all-consuming revenge. In that spirit, the novel ends not with Victor's death but, after this occurs, the disappearance of the monster, as he drifts into the savage landscape that is symbolic of Victor's ceaseless pursuit of his foe: the monster "sprang from the cabin-window as he said this, upon the ice raft which lay close to the vessel. He was soon borne away by the waves and lost in darkness and distance." Similar to Ulysses' intellectual shipwreck, Victor's scientific dream also leads to disaster, as it is engulfed by the natural sublime.

The Romantic era's passion for Dante was the most important chapter in the resurgence of the *Commedia* after its ups and downs in previous centuries, especially after the outright condemnation of Dante's writing by Enlightenment thinkers including the avowed secularist Voltaire and the Jesuit aesthete Saverio Bettinelli. The representations of Dante and his *Commedia* in Madame de Staël and Mary Shelley provide a representative view of three key tendencies of Dante's Romantic apotheosis: First, the increased secularization of Dante's explicitly Christian writing, to the point where doctrinal issues from *Paradiso* were almost entirely excluded from the interests of readers focused exclusively on *Inferno* and its psychological dramas (it was the rare Romantic who engaged either *Purgatorio* or *Paradiso*). Second, the burgeoning obsession with Dante the man and hero, both as protagonist of his poem and as the "last medieval" whose writing paved the way for the Renaissance. And third, the new popularity of Dante among previously marginalized groups, especially women writers like Madame de Staël and Shelley, who celebrated Dante's love of freedom at a time when men dominated the world of publishing to such a degree that Shelley's name was not even included on the title page of her masterpiece *Frankenstein*, a fate she shared with other leading female authors including Jane Austen.

When Stendhal proclaimed Dante "le poète romantique par excellence," he was not merely gesturing toward Dante's popularity. He was also suggesting, in a profound way, that Dante was a fellow Romantic. The *Commedia* became the mirror where many authors of the age, male and female, looked to find themselves reflected.

Chapter 6

Transition and Translation

WHILE MANY ROMANTIC authors were invested in the heroic persona of Dante, often to the exclusion of his *Commedia*'s religious content and formal innovations, a parallel chapter in the reception history of the poem also arose in the nineteenth century that had a profound impact on how we read it today: Dante's work was entering into its golden age of translation.[1] This phenomenon of "Dante tradotto" began during the early nineteenth century and therefore also bore a distinctly Romantic stamp. In keeping with the age's project of making literature less the exclusive domain of high culture and more a part of everyday life, important translations of the *Commedia* began to circulate in the early nineteenth century. Romantic renderings of Dante were not always felicitous: a blank-verse version of the poem by the Scottish surgeon and radical parliamentarian Joseph Hume from 1812 was described by the eminent *dantista* Paget Toynbee as "probably the worst translation of any portion of Dante's works ever published."[2] But on the whole this sudden energy in making Dante available in foreign languages and foreign editions was gathering considerable momentum. For it was during Romanticism that classic translations, notably Henry Francis Cary's *The Vision* from 1814, emerged to disseminate Dante's *Commedia* to broad swaths of non-Italian readers. The focus on translating Dante was transitional in that it represented a new collective interest in the formal construction of the *Commedia* as well as a movement away from an obsession with the plot of Dante's dramatic narrative and the psychological makeup of Dante himself, as both poet and protagonist. Just as Dante had urged his contemporaries to adopt the vernacular, many writers in the nineteenth century turned their energies toward translating Dante in hope of rendering him accessible to their own local cultures. Germaine de Staël said it best in her landmark essay on translation,[3] which inspired a series of polemical responses in Italy that helped usher in that nation's Romantic movement:

> The greatest service we can render literature is to transport the masterpieces of the human intellect from one language to another. So few truly great works exist, and genius of any kind whatsoever is so rare a phenomenon that each modern nation would always remain impoverished if it were reduced to its own treasures. Besides, more than any other form of exchange, the circulation of ideas is the one most likely to prove advantageous.[4]

Since the *Commedia* had long been considered canonical, it belonged to Madame de Staël's elite group of "truly great works" that cried out for translation. In a passage that evokes Dante's efforts on behalf of the vernacular, Madame de Staël notes, "Latin poets of the Middle Ages were translated into Italian by their countrymen, for it is much more natural to prefer a language that refers to the emotions of real life rather than one that can only be recreated through study!"[5] Just as Dante's vernacular was attuned to the rhythms and cadences of the everyday, so too did translations of his work speak to the "emotions of real life" for the non-Tuscan reader. A work in translation, she concluded, can bring a much more "intimate" pleasure than one read in a foreign language.[6] The message for Romantic authors was clear: for Dante's work truly to hit home, his words needed to appear in their own languages.

One author who heeded the translator's call was Byron. Like so many of his contemporaries, Byron was enthralled by the image of the Dantesque self, the hero who transcends trials and tribulations. His work was part of a broader engagement with Dante's version of the self that shaped the Romantic genre of autobiography. Unlike the more impersonal, restrained, and externally oriented Enlightenment memoir, Romantic autobiography—in the manner of the watershed *Confessions* by Jean-Jacques Rousseau (written in 1768 and published posthumously in 1783)—prized interiority, the mystery of personal identity, and the force of emotion. In looking for a literary model for their autobiographical projects, Romantics like Byron turned to Dante and his associated topoi of literary heroism, self-exploration, and artistic endurance in the face of strife. Byron's *The Prophecy of Dante* (1819), among other works of his, is filled with gestures toward the captivating persona of the Florentine poet. As Diego Saglia writes, "In Byron's case, Dante figured as one in a series of revered 'poets of action,' literary heroes who were 'brave and active citizens,' playing an active role in the public arena as opposed to the increasing contemporary exclusion of the poet from political intervention."[7] This personal connection was such that it is impossible to conceive of an adjective like "Byronic" without the precedent "Dantesque."[8]

Dantesque notions suffused Byron's understanding of his own self-exile, which included an extended sojourn in Italy.

Few poets are more synonymous with the myth of the exiled foreign artist in Italy than Byron, author of such memorable lines as "Italia! Oh Italia! thou who hast / The fatal gift of beauty."[9] Byron's representation of Italy in *Childe Harold's Pilgrimage* squares with some of the most standard—if not stereotypical—nineteenth-century foreign views on Italy: it is a place that has seen its better days, a "funeral dower of present woes and past"; it has an illustrious history, with "annals graved in characters of flame"; and it is a beautiful albeit weak female body politic in the allegorical sense, a centuries-old metaphor of Dantesque provenance ("Oh God! that thou wert in thy nakedness / Less lovely or more powerful").[10] Byron broke with Romantic clichés about Italy by employing a highly charged political rhetoric that transformed it into an outlier "feminine" nation that was rudely treated by supposedly more "masculine" European powers, especially France and Austria.[11] This Risorgimentalist, republican aspect to Byron's thinking on Italy made it natural that he would turn to Dante, a figure whom Romantics creatively misread as a crusader for democratic reform, even though his *Commedia* promoted ancient Roman imperial rule and his *De monarchia* celebrated autocracy.[12]

But it was not just Dante the "hero" who captured Byron's attention: he was also fascinated by the actual text of the *Commedia* and would prove to be one of its most compelling translators. His entry point into Dante, as with so much of Byron, passed through love and lust. "Few stories captured and held Byron's imagination as tenaciously as that of Francesca da Rimini," Frederick L. Beaty observed in 1960, and scholars continue to grapple with the ghostlike presence of Dante's star-crossed lover in Byron's poetry and thought.[13] Byron defended Dante's condemnation of the lustful in *Inferno* 5 against his contemporary Ugo Foscolo—the great poet and Dante scholar who emphasized the canto's level of pain and cruelty—by writing: "Who *but* Dante could have introduced any 'gentleness' at all into Hell?"[14] It is no wonder that Byron would be drawn to the tragic Francesca, who shared his attraction to forbidden love and raw emotion. Byron also shared much with Francesca's lover, Paolo: like Dante's silent shade, the English poet was rumored to have been involved with his half-sister, Augusta Leigh, the recipient of many an anguished letter from Bryon that contained references to *Inferno* 5.[15] Byron's interest in Francesca dated back to at least 1816, when he assisted Leigh Hunt in revising and publishing his *Story of Rimini*, a much-maligned work that Byron defended as "devilish good" in a letter from that same year.[16] Byron also alluded to the story of Francesca in other works from 1816, *Parisina* and *The Siege of Corinth*.

The culmination of Byron's passion for Dante and his star-crossed lovers was his translation of *Inferno* 5 on March 5, 1820:

"The Land where I was born sits by the Seas
Upon that shore to which the Po descends,
With all his followers, in search of peace.
Love, which the gentle heart soon apprehends,
Seized him for the fair person which was ta'en
From me, and me even yet the mode offends.
Love, who to none beloved to love again
Remits, seized me with wish to please, so strong,
That, as thou see'st, yet, yet it doth remain.
Love to one death conducted us along,
But Caina waits for him our life who ended:"
These were the accents uttered by her tongue.
—Since I first listened to these Souls offended,
I bowed my visage, and so kept it till—

"What think'st thou?" said the bard; when I unbended,
And recommenced: "Alas! unto such ill
How many sweet thoughts, what strong ecstacies,
Led these their evil fortune to fulfill!"
And then I turned unto their side my eyes,
And said, "Francesca, thy sad destinies
Have made me sorrow till the tears arise.
But tell me, in the Season of sweet sighs,
By what and how thy Love to Passion rose,
So as his dim desires to recognize?"
Then she to me: "The greatest of all woes
Is to remind us of our happy days
In misery, and that thy teacher knows.
But if to learn our Passion's first root preys
Upon thy spirit with such Sympathy,
I will do even as he who weeps and says.
We read one day for pastime, seated nigh,
Of Lancilot, how Love enchained him too.
We were alone, quite unsuspiciously.
But oft our eyes met, and our Cheeks in hue
All o'er discoloured by that reading were;
But one point only wholly us o'erthrew;
When we read the long-sighed-for smile of her,
To be thus kissed by such devoted lover,
He, who from me can be divided ne'er,
Kissed my mouth, trembling in the act all over:
Accurséd was the book and he who wrote!
That day no further leaf we did uncover."
While thus one Spirit told us of their lot,
The other wept, so that with Pity's thralls
I swooned, as if by Death I had been smote,
And fell down even as a dead body falls.

The passage represents Byron's most significant engagement with the *Commedia*. His Francesca was an example of how, in the words of one critic, British Romantics read Dante against the grain: Francesca may be in hell, but for Byron she was "not a damned, unrepentant soul, but rather a heroine who evoked pity, sympathy and indeed admiration."[17] Though there were many other Romantic translations of *Inferno* 5, most have been forgotten, and only a later version by the Pre-Raphaelite poet and painter Dante Gabriel Rossetti rivaled Byron's in quality.[18] Byron's translation succeeds in recreating the delicate music of Dante's original ("But tell me, in the Season of sweet sighs") and its confused erotic language ("Love, who to none beloved to love again / Remits"). Though Byron promised in his letters a "faithful" rendering of the canto, in truth he took liberties with the source, except in his metrical choice. His use of Dante's *terza rima*, always a challenge in rhyme-poor English, strove to match the pacing and rhythm of the original, in a meter that few others were able to employ skillfully.[19]

Despite its pretense of "accuracy," Byron's translation is actually "pervaded by his liberal Dantean poetics," as one commentator observed.[20] This politicization of Dante during the Romantic era was intense. As I have argued elsewhere,[21] when Wordsworth attacked Dante as a "religionist" poet, he was actually lashing out at the younger writers (like Shelley, Hazlitt, Keats, and Byron) who had made Dante their poetic hero. Byron in turn loathed Wordsworth, writing that his *Lyrical Ballads* volume was neither prose nor poetry, and its celebrated preface was "the very worst prose that ever was written."[22] Ultimately, Byron and Wordsworth stood a universe apart artistically and temperamentally, so it is no surprise that despite their mutual reservations about Dante's work as a whole, Byron would be drawn to a highly sexualized element of it that could never pique the interest of the more propriety-bound Wordsworth.

Byron's obsession with Francesca transcended the literary and extended into the personal. He went so far as to look for physical traces of her life in Rimini but was disappointed to find nothing, in part because there was little to discover: as has been noted, there was no record of Francesca's illicit love for Paolo before Dante's version of it in *Inferno* 5.[23] So Dante must have invented her out of hearsay, gossip, and his own fancy. How fitting, because for Byron, Francesca was above all a haunting figure of the imagination. After his translation of *Inferno* 5, in his *Ravenna Journals* from 1821, Byron announced his plans to write a play of his own on the subject of Paolo and Francesca.[24] This work would never come to pass. But Dante's Francesca continued to occupy much of Byron's thoughts, for Francesca—Byron's "unwritten lady"—was the literary-historical embodiment of forbidden love and irresistible temptation and thus a signature figure in Byron's poetics.

———

As important as Byron's translation of *Inferno* 5 was in revealing Romantic engagement with key technical aspects of the *Commedia*, especially *terza rima*, it paled in influence to the most significant of all nineteenth-century translations of Dante. This landmark work was not produced in Europe, the main site for engaging with the *Commedia*, but rather across the Atlantic in a literary culture that was channeling the Romantic energies of authors including Byron. In 1845, two decades after Byron's death in 1824, Henry Wadsworth Longfellow wrote "Mezzo Cammin," a combination of Dantesque homage and probing self-reflection:

Half of my life is gone, and I have let
The years slip from me and have not fulfilled
The aspiration of my youth, to build
Some tower of song with lofty parapet.
Not indolence, nor pleasure, nor the fret
Of restless passions that would not be stilled,
But sorrow, and a care that almost killed,
Kept me from what I may accomplish yet;
Though, half-way up the hill, I see the Past
Lying beneath me with its sounds and sights,—
A city in the twilight dim and vast,
With smoking roofs, soft bells, and gleaming lights,—
And hear above me on the autumnal blast
The cataract of Death far thundering from the heights.[25]

The words express concerns similar to those voiced by Milton centuries earlier in his sonnet "When I consider how my light is spent," a work that may have been influenced by Dante as well.[26] Longfellow's debt to Dante is spelled out explicitly, as the poem's title recapitulates the first line of Dante's poem ("When I had journeyed half of our life's way," *Nel mezzo del cammin di nostra vita, Inf.* 1.1).[27] A professor of Romance languages at Harvard and a well-regarded poet, Longfellow had not yet produced that one great work ("Some tower of song with lofty parapet") that he expected of himself. Part of the reason was his lofty academic position: he felt that the demands of teaching were absorbing energies that could have gone into writing. Another part of the problem was what he called "a care that almost killed": the death of his first wife, Mary Powell, just a year into their marriage. Though Longfellow could not have known it at the time, he would indeed achieve that elusive greatness, and Dante would be at the center of it—though only after experiencing an even greater sorrow that would, once again, nearly kill him.

The aspirations conjured by Longfellow in "Mezzo Cammin" square perfectly with the image of Dante that Longfellow created that same year with his eponymous poem "Dante":

> Tuscan, that wanderest through the realms of gloom,
> With thoughtful pace, and sad, majestic eyes,
> Stern thoughts and awful from thy soul arise,
> Like Farinata from his fiery tomb.
> Thy sacred song is like the trump of doom;
> Yet in thy heart what human sympathies,
> What soft compassion glows, as in the skies
> The tender stars their clouded lamps relume!
> Methinks I see thee stand, with pallid cheeks
> By Fra Hilario in his diocese,
> As up the convent-walls, in golden streaks,
> The ascending sunbeams mark the day's decrease;
> And, as he asks what there the stranger seeks,
> Thy voice along the cloister whispers, "Peace!"

We are once again in the Romantic terrain of Vittorio Alfieri, Thomas Carlyle, Thomas Babington Macaulay, and the host of other predecessors whose topos of the heroic Dante was much closer in personality to the sinners of hell than the blessed in heaven, as we see in Longfellow's description of Farinata, the great Ghibelline general who rises from his fiery tomb "as if he had tremendous scorn for Hell" (com' avesse l'inferno a gran dispitto, Inf. 10.36). The epic inflections the poem are apt, for in Longfellow's New England the Romantic version of Dante as visionary was everywhere. Longfellow's friend and fellow Bostonian Ralph Waldo Emerson had translated Dante's Vita nuova in 1843 and had gone on to hail Dante as a "new and prodigious person" whom American writers should take as their model.[28] Margaret Fuller continued the Romantic interest in Dante by women writers by scouring the *Vita nuova* for its "intuitions as to the *new life of love.*"[29] And authors on the level of Nathaniel Hawthorne, Herman Melville, and Walt Whitman all vigorously read and commented upon the *Commedia*.[30] Dante's American arrival was confirmed.

As important as these other writers were, it was above all Longfellow who put Dante on the American literary map. He had been lecturing on the poet for decades, beginning in 1836 at Harvard and up to his retirement in 1855, when he left academia so that he could focus on his writing. More important, he had begun translating the *Commedia* as early as 1843, working on his favorite canticle, *Purgatorio*. He would not finish his translation of it until 1853, and for the next several years he barely returned to the project. Then a profound disaster struck that would return him to the *Commedia* for good—and place him on the road to creating that "tower of song with lofty parapet" that would guarantee his immortality.

On July 10, 1861, Longfellow's wife, Fanny, cut their seven-year-old daughter Edith's hair and decided to preserve the curls in a sealed envelope. What followed remains a mystery: perhaps a few drops of the wax fell on Fanny's dress and ignited; perhaps an errant candle accidentally dripped onto Fanny's clothing to set it ablaze; or perhaps the blaze was caused by children playing with matches.[31] Whatever the cause, Fanny's highly flammable muslin dress burst into flame. Longfellow threw himself onto his wife and desperately tried to put out the fire, burning his hands badly. But his wife lost consciousness and never recovered. She died later that day.

The word *grief* does not fully capture the emotional devastation that followed. Friends spoke of Longfellow as "raving" and frightened of being "sent to an asylum."[32] The most famous poet in America and a bestselling author, he was lost without Fanny, his soulmate, first reader, and lifelong love. He had spent seven years courting her before they wed, and their happy union produced six children. A month after her death, on August 18, 1861, Longfellow wrote, with typical understatement and equanimity, "How I am alive after what my eyes have seen, I know not. I am at least patient, if not resigned; and thank God hourly—as I have from the beginning—for the beautiful life we led together, and that I loved her more and more to the end."[33] Only eighteen years later, in his poem "The Cross of Snow," did he give full vent to his sorrow:

> In the long, sleepless watches of the night,
> A gentle face—the face of one long dead—
> Looks at me from the wall, where round its head
> The night-lamp casts a halo of pale light.
> Here in this room she died, and soul more white
> Never through martyrdom of fire was led
> To its repose; nor can in books be read
> The legend of a life more benedight.
> There is a mountain in the distant West
> That, sun-defying, in its deep ravines
> Displays a cross of snow upon its side.
> Such is the cross I wear upon my breast
> These eighteen years, through all the changing scenes
> And seasons, changeless since the day she died.

The wrenching image of a man bearing an invisible cross of sorrow for two full decades—incidentally enough, the length of Dante's exile—recalls Sigmund Freud's brutal insight on grief as the ultimate "invisible" illness.[34]

After Fanny's death, Dante's *Commedia* went from being an ongoing concern of Longfellow's to a daily obsession. In the words of one scholar, Longfellow "soon became absorbed in his Dante and received new courage from communing with him."[35] Comparing Dante's *Commedia* to a vast cathedral, Longfellow wrote, "I enter here from day to day / And leave my burden at the minister gate."[36] The work was both balm and burden: he soon discovered that working on the translation made it difficult to focus on his original compositions, as he committed himself to publishing the entire *Commedia* and became obsessed with its revision. Harvard luminaries including the medievalist Charles Eliot Norton, the poet James Russell Lowell, and the writer William Dean Howells all convened at their friend Longfellow's home to hear him read from his Dante translations and offer their counsel. Thus was the "Dante Club" born.[37]

Longfellow was typically modest about his translation: "The only merit my book has is that it is exactly what Dante says, and not what the translator imagines he might have said if he had been an Englishman . . . while making it rhythmic, I have endeavored to make it also as literal as a prose translation."[38] Despite their simplicity, these words speak volumes, suggesting how and why Longfellow remains arguably the most important translator of Dante in the history of American literature. To understand fully his achievement, one must first take a step back and consider the challenges that Dante presents to the translator of English. As I have argued elsewhere, his deeply idiomatic, rhyme-rich Tuscan and cascading *terza rima*, which give the poem its vaulting energy, are well-nigh impossible to reproduce in rhyme-poor English.[39] As we have seen, only uniquely talented poets on the order of Byron and Shelley managed to re-create Dante's meter to positive effect.[40] The content of Dante's writing also presents formidable obstacles to translators: he filled his verses with allusions to ancient, biblical, and contemporary medieval writing while tackling a wide array of issues across the intellectual disciplines and creating hundreds of literary personae, some based on people he knew and some whom he invented.[41] For all these reasons, the expert translator of Dante must be *both* poet and scholar, capable of rendering his literary qualities while also grasping his profound level of erudition.[42]

Longfellow checked both boxes. His work on the Romance languages and Dante had earned him the most prestigious academic position in Italian literature in the land, at Harvard. He spoke multiple languages, including Tuscan/Italian, and he was an active translator throughout his career, not just from Italian but also Spanish. These scholarly skills, combined with his prodigious faculties as America's most revered poet, were brought to bear on his translation of the *Commedia*. His commitment to rendering Dante "literally" (which has had its critics)[43] resulted in a close translation that feels tethered by invisible strings to Dante's Tuscan, setting the source and target language into a sustained dialogue that drives his rendition from the first line to the last.[44]

Longfellow's vigorous commitment to Dante's original text is evident in his translation of the celebrated inscription on the Gates of Hell in *Inferno* 3. His English barely budges from the Tuscan, to the point where his syntactic and lexical choices give his version an awkward and non-idiomatic feel:

> "Through me the way is to the city dolent:
> Through me the way is to eternal dole;
> Through me the way among the people lost."

> *"Per me si va ne la città dolente,*
> *per me si va ne l'etterno dolore,*
> *per me si va tra la perduta gente."* (1–3)

Longfellow's archaic *dolent* in line 1 recalls its Latin root *dolens* ("suffering, in pain"), while nearly reproducing verbatim Dante's *dolente*. Similarly, his *eternal dole* in line 2 matches Dante's *etterno dolore*, while interlacing tightly with the concluding words of the first and third verses (*dolent / dole / lost*) in a rhythmic pattern that approximates the rhyming flow of Dante's *terza rima*. Here as elsewhere, Longfellow goes so deeply into the *Commedia*'s verbal warp and woof that the reader can feel his English being refashioned by Dante's Tuscan.

Longfellow's translation of the *Commedia* had an immediate, indelible success. The appearance of his *Inferno* coincided with the six hundredth anniversary of Dante's birth and the establishment of Florence as Italy's capital in 1865. Not surprisingly, Longfellow's translation was sent to the Italian committee in charge of the celebrations. His *Purgatorio* appeared in 1866 and *Paradiso* the following year. By 1867, American readers had access to a work that distilled a lifetime of Longfellow's investment in Dante, the ultimate literary monument to a Dante *americanizzato*—fully Americanized. In the words of one scholar, the influence of Longfellow's project cannot be overstated, for "the fact that the most famous and popular of all the American poets of the time turned his talents to making a translation of the *Divine Comedy* was a potent factor in inducing American readers to strike up an acquaintance with the great poem."[45]

Twenty years after Longfellow's translation, the poet found himself once again at the center of Dante's American rebirth. The Dante Society of America, a direct offshoot of that original Dante Club that had gathered in Longfellow's home to hear his Dante translations, was founded in 1881 through the leadership of Longfellow, Lowell, and Norton, who in turn served as its first three presidents. To this day, the society's mission is to encourage the study and appreciation of the time, life, works, and cultural legacy of Dante Alighieri. The oldest scholarly association for the study of Dante in the country, it has occasionally met on 105 Brattle Street in Cambridge, Massachusetts, a site that contains its fair share of Dante memorabilia—and was once the home of Longfellow and his beloved wife Fanny.

Chapter 7

The Modernist Dante

S'io credesse che mia risposta fosse
A persona che mai tornasse al mondo,
Questa fiamma staria senza piu scosse.
Ma perciocche giammai di questo fondo
Non torno vivo alcun, s'i'odo il vero,
Senza tema d'infamia ti rispondo.

THUS BEGINS a poem, an *English* poem no less, that incorporates Dante's famous lines from *Inferno* 27 in their original and untranslated Tuscan. T. S. Eliot's "The Love Song of J. Alfred Prufrock" from 1915 is considered an early harbinger of High Modernism, a movement that Dante would be central to, just as he was essential to Eliot personally.[1] In Eliot's words, Dante "had the most persistent and deepest influence upon [my] own verse."[2] He also remarked that *Paradiso* was "the highest point that poetry has ever reached or can reach."[3] According to Eliot, Dante was the eminently "European" poet because his poetic lessons were ones all on the Continent could take to heart. Similarly, Eliot believed that Dante was the greatest "religious" poet because he "expresses everything in the way of emotion, between depravity's despair and the beatific vision, that man is capable of experiencing."[4]

These oracular statements, coming from late in Eliot's career, reveal Dante's impact on works ranging from *The Waste Land* (1922) to *Little Gidding* (1942), the fourth and final poem of his *Four Quartets* (1943). "The Love Song of J. Alfred Prufrock" was written much earlier, as Eliot completed its initial draft in 1911 when he was only twenty-two. Yet the poem comes across not as the work of a young man but rather as a song of weariness, apprehension, inertia, and superannuation. Its verses stand a world apart from the verve and bravado of the Byronic hero and the loquacious monster created ex nihilo in Mary Shelley's *Frankenstein*. No Romantic protagonist worth his salt would have uttered a line like:

> I grow old . . . I grow old . . .
> I shall wear the bottoms of my trousers rolled.
> Shall I part my hair behind? Do I dare to eat a peach?
> ("The Love Song of J. Alfred Prufrock," 120–22)[5]

Astonishingly, Dante's verse could fuel the impassioned eloquence of Mary Shelley's Victor Frankenstein as he exhorted a crew of sailors to pursue the monster *and* the involuted paralysis of T. S. Eliot's narrator as he contemplates as anodyne an act as parting his hair or eating a piece of fruit. The references by Shelley to Dante's Ulysses from *Inferno* 26 and by Eliot to Guido da Montefeltro in *Inferno* 27 both point to one of the greatest rhetorical relations in all of the *Commedia*: the descent from Ulysses' "epic" and "tragic" grandiloquence to Guido's "comic" speech.[6] More broadly, the linguistic slide from the Romantic invocation of Ulysses to the Modernist citation of Guido da Montefeltro reveals a changing understanding of the *Commedia's* place in literary culture. As we will see, the transition from Mary Shelley's

Ulysses to T. S. Eliot's Guido da Montefeltro marks a move away from the Romantic obsession with Dante's persona to the Modernist investment in his experimental poetics.

Despite his obvious moral flaws, Mary Shelley's Victor Frankenstein is a larger-than-life genius and creator. It comes as no surprise that, in a moment of need, he reaches out for the words of another deeply flawed, supremely gifted hero, the epic Ulysses, one of the most memorable characters in all of Dante's hell. Channeling Ulysses' eloquence, Victor's speech is pitched consistently high ("Oh! Be men, or be more than men"), reflecting the general Romantic preference for what Thomas Carlyle called the "heroic" Dante: the protagonist who seems to supplant his own poem (as Carlyle writes, "so could the Hero [Dante], in his forsakeness, in his extreme need, still say to himself: 'Follow thou thy star, thou shalt not fail of a glorious haven!'").[7]

A Modernist in the making like Eliot in "Prufrock" was after different Dantesque quarry. The opening reference to Guido's words is untranslated because, unlike the Romantics, who aimed at emotional authenticity and affective connection with their readers, Eliot and his fellow Modernists wished to separate sophisticated literary production from mainstream cultural consumption—in this regard one might think of them as latter-day Petrarchans. Difficulty and complexity, distilled in the trademark stream-of-consciousness style that suffuses "Prufrock" and the work of contemporaries like James Joyce and Virginia Woolf, were the aesthetic buzzwords of the Modernist movement, pushing its adherents to chart new artistic ground even if the output risked lapsing into the opaque and unintelligible—which is why works like Joyce's *Ulysses* (1922) and Eliot's *The Waste Land* are so difficult to read without a guide. To access a poem like Eliot's "Prufrock," one does well to know the predecessor texts that inspired him as well as the languages, foreign and native, that permeated his consciousness. The difference between the Romantic and Modernist Dante informs Eliot's syntax. His epigraph cites the words of Guido da Montefeltro, a notorious and immoral political operator, during his encounter with Dante the pilgrim in the Circle of False Counselors. With typical brio, Guido offers Dante what is likely the first (and perhaps only) triple subjunctive in literary history:

> "*If I thought* my reply *were meant* for one
> who *ever could return* into the world,
> this flame *would stir* no more . . ."

> "*S'i'* credesse *che mia risposta* fosse
> *a persona che mai* tornasse *al mondo,*
> *questa fiamma* staria *sanza più scosse . . .*" (emphasis added;
>   *Inf.* 27.61–63)

To underscore the passage's rhetorical sophistication, I highlight the three subjunctive verbs in the first two lines of the tercet—distinguished in Italian by their hissing -*s* sounds (*credesse, fosse, tornasse*)—as well as the conditional verb in the third line (*staria*), which signals Guido's decision to allow himself to speak to the pilgrim based on the premises of his hypotheticals. Typical of hell, Guido is ingenious in his particular assumptions, yet also wrong in his general thinking. Contrary to Guido's conclusion, Dante will in fact "return into the world" from hell, as would others from the realms of religion (Jesus, Adam) and literature (Aeneas, Odysseus/Ulysses). Dante wishes to emphasize, as Eliot brilliantly intuited, how the consciousness of the arch-conniver and über-schemer Guido is structured in linguistic knots, mazes, and labyrinths. He is the ultimate backroom operator who sells his words and actions to the highest bidder. His language thus articulates a series of hedged bets predicated on hiding the cards he has been dealt and hopes to redistribute to his advantage.

Protagonist of the eponymous poem, Eliot's Prufrock is fully a creature of the subjunctive. The poem is everywhere a disavowal of agency and direct action; Prufrock's tutelary deity would seem to be the prince of indecision, Hamlet. But Eliot rejects even that option as too grand:

> No! I am not Prince Hamlet, nor was meant to be;
> Am an attendant lord, one that will do
> To swell a progress, start a scene or two,
> Advise the prince; no doubt, an easy tool,
> Deferential, glad to be of use,
> Politic, cautious, and meticulous;
> Full of high sentence, but a bit obtuse;
> At times, indeed, almost ridiculous—
> Almost, at times, the Fool. (111–19)

Eliot's everyman (a mere "attendant lord") is a far cry from the Romantic superman. As Eliot explained, his rejection of the Romantic cult of the individual, and by extension the topos of the heroic Dante that it engendered, was woven into the very fiber of Modernist poetics:

> What is to be insisted upon is that the poet must develop or procure the consciousness of the past and that he should continue to develop this consciousness throughout his career. What happens is a continual surrender of himself as he is at the moment to something which is more valuable. The progress of an artist is a continual self-sacrifice, a continual extinction of personality. There remains to define this

process of depersonalization and its relation to the sense of tradition. It is in this depersonalization that art may be said to approach the condition of science.[8]

The negative correlation of Eliot's words to Romantic principles is astonishing. While one might find echoes in Eliot of what Keats famously called "negative capability"—as well as Keats's related remark that "the Poet is the most unpoetical of any thing in existence; because he has no Identity"[9]—the general tenor of Eliot's discussion is to reject the Romantic emphasis on the self and move into a more depersonalized realm. In a testament to the variety of readings that Dante could inspire, the *Commedia*, which had served to bolster the self in the Romantic age, became in Eliot's Modernist age a vehicle for occluding it. As Eliot writes, "for my meaning is, that the poet has, not a 'personality' to express, but a particular medium, which is only a medium and not a personality, in which impressions and experiences combine in peculiar and unexpected ways."[10] Eliot thus chose the speech from *Inferno* 27 in "Prufrock" not because of Guido's extravagant, captivating persona but rather as the linguistic code that anticipates the thematic and affective claims of his poem. In less than seventy-five years, the Romantics had lifted the *Commedia* out of its Enlightenment doldrums and made it their sacred source of selfhood and the unbridled imagination. With no less drama (and in less than a hundred years), Modernists like Eliot had depersonalized the Dantesque self and transformed the formal innovations of his *Commedia* into the DNA of their poetics.

In a memorial service for Eliot at his alma mater, Harvard, in 1965, the Milton scholar Douglas Bush divided Eliot's career into three Dantesque periods, with *The Waste Land* as his *Inferno*, *Ash Wednesday* as his *Purgatorio*, and *Four Quartets* as his *Paradiso*.[11] Allusions to Dante in all of these works are indeed abundant, with implications that extend well beyond the poetic and into the spiritual. After his conversion from Unitarianism to Anglo-Catholicism in 1927, Eliot became increasingly interested in the doctrinal details of the *Commedia*. To cite just one example of how poetic and religious elements fuse in Eliot's relation to Dante, in *Little Gidding*—arguably the most Christian of all of Eliot's works—the narrator describes a meeting indebted to one of the most heart-rending in all of *Inferno*, Dante's encounter with his former mentor, Brunetto Latini, who like the character in *Little Gidding* suffers under a rain of fire that scorch his features in canto 15. Eliot writes:

> ... in the waning dusk
> I caught the sudden look of some dead master
> Whom I had known, forgotten, half recalled
> Both one and many: in the brown baked features
> The eyes of a familiar compound ghost
> Both intimate and unidentifiable
> So I assumed a double part, and cried
> And heard another's voice cry, "What! are you here?"
> (2.718–25)[12]

The lines from the stranger directly echo Dante's words in finding his long-lost mentor in hell: ("Are you here, Ser Brunetto?," "*Siete voi qui, Ser Brunetto?*," *Inf.* 15.30). The haunting phrase "compound ghost" seems to sum up Dante's presence in Eliot, which, according to Eliot's own words from 1950, was so pervasive as to be indescribable:

> I do not think I can explain everything [about my debt to Dante]; but as I still, after forty years, regard his poetry as the most persistent and deepest influence upon my own verse, I should like to establish at least some of the reasons for it.[13]

A fitting homage expressed in Dante's own beloved topos of ineffability, Eliot's words suggest how the *Commedia* represented a poetic almanac and spiritual diary in one.

———

Eliot was one of many Modernists enthralled by the *Commedia*. Dante's epic informed the work of almost all of the noteworthy poets associated with the movement, from Eliot and Ezra Pound to W. H. Auden and W. B. Yeats.[14] The latter's poem "Ego Dominus Tuus" distills what Dante had come to mean for the Modernist project. The title is taken from Dante's *Vita nuova*: they are the words spoken to Dante by the personified figure of Love after the young poet falls under the spell of his muse, Beatrice. Yeats's poem assumes the form of a dialogue between the pragmatic *Hic* (Latin for "this man") and the idealist *Ille* ("that man," and according to Pound a shorthand for "Willie" or William Butler Yeats), who believes that the glorious past has become disconnected from a debased present. In the words of one critic, the true aim of the poem is to steer the argument toward a "defense of the theory of an 'anti-self' on aesthetic rather than on psychological grounds,"[15] a view articulated by Yeats in these prophetic lines:

> That is our modern hope, and by its light
> We have lit upon the gentle, sensitive mind
> And lost the old nonchalance of the hand;
> Whether we have chosen chisel, pen or brush,
> We are but critics, or but half create,
> Timid, entangled, empty and abashed,
> Lacking the countenance of our friends. (12–18)[16]

The poem appeared in 1918 and reflected on the issue of depersonalization that interested Eliot. In a similar vein, Yeats writes:

Hic. And yet
The chief imagination of Christendom,
Dante Alighieri, so utterly found himself
That he has made that hollow face of his
More plain to the mind's eye than any face
But that of Christ.
Ille. And did he find himself
Or was the hunger that had made it hollow
A hunger for the apple on the bough
Most out of reach? and is that spectral image
The man that Lapo and that Guido knew?
I think he fashioned from his opposite
An image that might have been a stony face
Staring upon a Bedouin's horse-hair roof
From doored and windowed cliff, or half upturned
Among the coarse grass and the camel-dung.
He set his chisel to the hardest stone.
Being mocked by Guido for his lecherous life,
Derided and deriding, driven out
To climb that stair and eat that bitter bread,
He found the unpersuadable justice, he found
The most exalted lady loved by a man. (19–40)

Whereas *Hic* posits an identity between Dante the man and artist—a move typical of readers of the *Commedia* ever since its Romantic resurgence—the more skeptical *Ille* sees Dante's work as transcending his own self, that is, as a "hunger for the apple on the bough / Most out of reach" and a pursuit of both "unpersuadable justice" and the "most exalted lady loved by a man."[17] Through what Auden described as Yeats's relentless inquiry into "the relation of Life and Art," Dante's personality for Yeats becomes absorbed by the larger, lyrical structures that it generated. The ensuing poetic forms then serve to consign the poet's actual persona—to quote Auden once more—into the "music" of history.[18] The intricacies of Yeats's lines reveal a deep knowledge of Dante's life and work, from the references to Guido Cavalcanti's poetic critique of Dante for his "lecherous life" to the indelible image of Dante the exile being forced "to climb that stair and eat that bitter bread."[19] Whereas Eliot's more acerbic reading of Romanticism posited a clean divide between the self and literary form, with Yeats we arrive at what one scholar describes as a Dante who is a sort of perfected Romantic, thus "realizing the romantics' goals while avoiding their supposed failures in execution."[20]

Despite the thematic weight that Dante bore in Yeats's understanding of literary history, his overt allusions and references to Dante's *Commedia* are relatively few. The same cannot be said for the man who, alongside Eliot, did more than any other early twentieth-century poet to further Dante's reputation and inscribe the *Commedia* into the cultural conversation. Ezra Pound's erratic, troubling personality has been well documented, as the once-caring mentor of countless young artists (Hemingway described him as "the most generous writer I have ever known")[21] became a raving fascist, anti-Semite, and Nazi sympathizer in his advancing age, resulting in his arrest, imprisonment, and diagnosis of mental disorder. Before this devastating conclusion, he was one of most important Modernist poets and arguably the most knowledgeable commentator on Dante in the creative world. His encyclopedic understanding of the *Commedia* and Dante's medieval age extended to the poet's circle, as he produced groundbreaking translations of Dante's *primo amico*, Guido Cavalcanti, even setting some of his poetry to music. Bold and extravagant in his views, he was never one to resist a provocative remark: "Dante's god is ineffable divinity," he once wrote. "Milton's god is a fussy old man with a hobby."[22]

Pound was fully aligned with his friend Eliot's view that Dante's poetry, and not his persona, was the proper focus: "It is tremendously important that great poetry be written, it makes no jot of difference who writes it. The experimental demonstrations of one man may save the time of many," he wrote in the essay "A Retrospect" in 1912, anticipating—and influencing—Eliot's views on artistic depersonalization by several years (Eliot actually edited the volume in which Pound's essay appeared).[23] Pound's immersion in the raw linguistic material of Dante's universe is evidenced by his sustained meditation on *De vulgari eloquentia*, a little-studied text that became Pound's guide to the *Commedia*. Following Dante's practice in *De vulgari eloquentia*, he offered elaborate classifications of individual words while drawing attention to their rhetorical structures, as we see in his analysis of the well-known opening image of the "dark wood" (*selva oscura*) from *Inferno* 1:

> Epithets may also be distinguished as epithets of primary and secondary apparition. By epithets of primary apparition I mean those which describe what is actually presented to the sense or vision. Thus in *selva oscura*, "shadowy wood"; epithets of secondary apparition or afterthought are such as in "sage Hippotades" or "forbidden tree" . . . there are also epithets of "emotional apparition," transensuous, suggestive: thus in Mr. Yeats' line "Under a bitter black wind that blows from the left hand" . . . [24]

Here we see the "philological Dante" of Modernist poetics, as Pound's reading explores the semantic and etymological inflections of Dante's writing and luxuriates in its rhetoric. The journey of Dante as Romantic hero had, by Pound's time, become a moot point, as the textual universe of the *Commedia* and its formal innovations became the primary locus of Modernist inquiry. It is telling that Pound discusses Dante here in the context of a contemporary poet like Yeats: for Pound, Eliot, and their circle, Dante was very much a "contemporary," a fellow poet whose work held magical forms and techniques worth studying over a lifetime because, to quote Pound, "at every stage of maturing—and that should be one's whole life—you are able to understand [a poet like Dante] better."[25]

No study of the Modernist Dante would be complete without mention of James Joyce. According to his biographer Richard Ellmann, Joyce's favorite writer was Dante.[26] It would be impossible to overstate the Irish novelist's affinity for the Florentine poet: his engagement with Dante's work was sustained and lifelong, as was his study of the Italian language. In Trieste, the first of his many exilic homes, he allegedly told his private students that "Italian literature begins with Dante and finishes with Dante.... In Dante dwells the whole spirit of the Renaissance. I love Dante almost as much as the Bible. He is my spiritual food."[27] Allusions to Dante permeate Joyce's work, covering a range of expressive registers and aesthetic functions, from the linguistically arcane and thematically weighted to the emotionally grave and even enigmatically playful. An especially mysterious and, I believe, self-mockingly ludic reference that suggests Dante's centrality to Joyce appears in his autobiographical *A Portrait of the Artist as a Young Man* from 1916, a work that bears striking parallels to Dante's *Vita nuova*. Both are artistic coming-of-age stories and exude a deep sense of self-nominated mission that could come across as arrogant—but would also prove to be prophetic. Soon before Joyce's alter ego Stephen Dedalus's departure from Ireland in *A Portrait of the Artist as a Young Man*, he annoys Emma Cleary, who like Dante's Beatrice is the subject of the young artist's idealized love, by opening before her skeptical eyes "the spiritual heroic refrigerating apparatus, invented and patented in all countries by Dante Alighieri."[28] One critic observed that this cryptic reference to Dante—so coded in fact that another more literal-minded scholar described it as a "puzzle unknown to cryologists" (experts in refrigeration)—suggests how the young Stephen is playfully yet pointedly invoking Dante as the "model for his self-preserving, exilic mode of emotional alienation."[29]

In Joyce's engagement with Dante, *Ulysses* represents the high-water mark. As Piero Boitani notes, "Quotations and misquotations from Dante fill *Ulysses* to the brim, and there is even some reason to think that the most elusive, ever-recurring character in the book, Macintosh, 'that lankylooking galoot,' might be Dante himself."[30] Boitani adds that though the structure of Ulysses is overtly—if loosely—Homeric, the "encyclopedialike spirit" of Dante permeates the poem, lending credence to Joyce's own admission of how intently he inhabited Dante's work while composing his great novel.[31] Looking back on writing *Ulysses* during World War I, Joyce remarked, "Ah, how wonderful that was to get up in the morning . . . and enter the misty regions of my emerging epic, as Dante once entered his selva oscura selva selvaggia. Words crackled in my head and a multitude of images crowded around, like those shades at the entrance to the Underworld when Ulysses stood there awaiting the spirit of Tiresias."[32] The juxtaposition of Dantesque and Homeric influences recalls the words of another author beloved by Joyce, a model for his robust linguistic experimentation in *Finnegans Wake* (1939): Giambattista Vico, who had referred to Dante as the Tuscan Homer.[33]

As we see in the celebrated stream of consciousness opening of Episode 3 in *Ulysses*, Dante permeates Joyce's literary—and Stephen Dedalus's fictional—consciousness:

Ineluctable modality of the visible: at least that if no more, thought through my eyes. Signatures of all things I am here to read, seaspawn and seawrack, the nearing tide, that rusty boot. Snotgreen, bluesilver, rust: coloured signs. Limits of the diaphane. But he adds: in bodies. Then he was aware of them bodies before of them coloured. How? By knocking his sconce against them, sure. Go easy. Bald he was and a millionaire, *maestro di color che sanno.* Limit of the diaphane in. Why in? Diaphane, adiaphane. If you can put your five fingers through it it is a gate, if not a door. Shut your eyes and see.[34]

The mention of "maestro di color che sanno" refers to Dante's catalogue of the great minds of antiquity in Limbo, where Aristotle is singled out as "the master of the men who know" (*Inf.* 4.131). The key is not so much the *what* of this allusion, its meaning or thematic weight, but the *how*, or manner in which Joyce makes the reference. The mention of Dante's Limbo is fleeting, in passing, and not meant to stall or halt the reader into elaborate interpretations. It aims instead to signal how Stephen's mind works. His musings range from the abstract and philosophical ("Ineluctable modality of the visible") to the visceral ("Snotgreen, bluesilver, rust: coloured signs") and ethereal ("Limit of the diaphane"). As the book progresses, there will be endless modulations in Stephen's stream of consciousness, including his tendency toward the explicitly sexual, as we see in the notorious Episode 13, with Leopold Bloom pleasuring himself at the sight of Gerty MacDowall's knickers, and Episode 15, when Bloom and Stephen visit Bella Cohen's brothel. Through all this diversity of perception, Dante remains a fixed point in Stephen's thinking and feeling, at times becoming the oxygen of his atmospheric range of cultural expressions. From the self-imposed exile of the young Stephen Dedalus in *A Portrait of the Artist as a Young Man* to the Latinate wordplays indebted to Dante's vernacular experimentalism in *Finnegans Wake*, Joyce remained one of Dante's most devoted heirs.

The final words to Joyce's masterpiece are the geographical markers "Trieste–Zurich–Paris," along with the dates of composition "1914–1921."[35] The completion of the book in the six-hundredth anniversary year of Dante's death was a felicitous coincidence that further cemented the link between these two epic authors. But the inclusion of the cities of composition suggests Dante's influence beyond mere serendipity. Joyce had chosen the life of the exiled author in large part because of Dante's precedent, wishing, as he famously announced toward the end of *A Portrait of the Artist as a Young Man*, "to forge in the smithy of my soul the uncreated conscience of my race."[36] He aimed to write of his Dublin at a distance and with the absolute freedom that only exile could bring, just as Dante had done with Florence. The insertion of "Trieste–Zurich–Paris" after Molly Bloom's concluding stream of consciousness signals the exilic points in which the book was written and renders palpable Joyce's embrace of Dante's outsider poetics and perspective. The Modernist *Commedia* took many forms, from its embodiment of Eliot's poetic "tradition" that overwhelmed any legacies of the Dantesque Romantic self to Pound's philological treasure house of linguistic forms and rhetorical experimentation indebted to the *Commedia*. In the concluding words of *Ulysses*, Dante's ghost resurfaces to haunt Joyce's lifelong quest to abandon his homeland and fire the literary tools of his soul's smithy.

Chapter 8

On Heroes and Hero-Worship

MUCH AS MODERNISTS like T. S. Eliot and Ezra Pound tried to root out the heroic Dante celebrated by Romantic authors and replace him with more careful attention to the verbal elements of Dante's text, the afterlife of Dante's poetic persona proved remarkably resilient.[1] Part of the reason was literary: writers on the self, from memoirists like Alfieri to poets on the order of Byron, had created indelible autobiographical models based on Dante. But part of the reason for Dante's ongoing cult of personality had as much to do with the events of the world as it did with the printed page. The first half of the twentieth century in Europe was a time of almost indescribable upheaval, as world war, genocide, and political revolution roiled the Continent, affecting all areas of life. Not surprisingly, Dante's legacy as a poet of civil discord and profound personal crisis that included exile and displacement figured centrally in this fractious era.

In the dramatic case of Primo Levi, Dante's *Commedia* could even become essential to survival. While Mussolini's ally Hitler ratcheted his anti-Semitic policies to insane levels in the 1930s, the Jewish Levi had no particular reason to fear that the Nazi sickness would spill into Italy. Despite the prejudices that they faced, Italian Jews had been allowed to live relatively peaceful lives since the Middle Ages, when the first Jewish settlement, the *ghetto*, was formed in Venice. But as Italy continued to founder in World War II and as the Fascists increasingly played supplicant to the Nazis in the Axis Pact, Hitler was able to force Mussolini's hand. In 1938, Mussolini instituted the Racial Laws that initiated the widespread persecution of the Italian Jews, described by Giorgio Bassani in his masterpiece, *Il giardino dei Finzi-Contini* (The garden of the Finzi-Continis, 1958). Five years later, in 1943, the fall of Mussolini's Fascist government plunged Italy into a civil war between the Nazi-backed supporters of Mussolini, who set up a puppet government in the northern Italian city of Salò, and the pro-democracy Italian partisans, whose ranks Levi joined. On December 14, 1943, Levi and his ragtag troop were captured by the German Gestapo in the Italian Alps and transported to Fossoli, one of the first Italian concentration camps. Three months later, Levi was loaded into a cattle car and shipped to Auschwitz, where the number 174517 was branded on his skin. Of the 650 prisoners in his cohort, only twenty were living when the Russian army liberated the camp a year later.

Levi's decisive encounter with Dante occurred in the most harrowing setting imaginable: Auschwitz, where the interred Levi met a fellow prisoner called Jean Samuel, a Frenchman from the border town of Alsace who was fluent in both French and German. Samuel served as the camp's "Pikolo," German-Italian slang for the "little guy" or "messenger boy"—the intermediary between the guards of the Nazi chemical plant at Auschwitz and the prisoners, including Levi, who worked there as slaves. Levi admired the calm, decency, physical strength, and studious air of the young Alsatian. One day, Pikolo tapped him for a coveted task: together, they would walk to the "Essenholen," the cafeteria, to retrieve the prisoners' meager rations. The job allowed for a full hour of daytime walking and fresh air in the prisoner's otherwise brutal regimen. En route, Levi and Samuel discovered their common love of books and study, which led to talk, of all things, of motherhood. Levi writes:

> . . . how all mothers resemble one another! His mother, too, had scolded him for never knowing how much money he had in his pocket; his mother, too, would have been amazed if she had known he had made it, that day by day he was making it.[2]

After this flash of genetic connection, Levi inexplicably recalled a line of poetry that he had long memorized, the famous words of Dante's Ulysses in *Inferno* 26.118–20:

> Consider well the seed that gave you birth:
> you were not made to live your lives as brutes,
> but to be followers of worth and knowledge.[3]

Such was the force of Ulysses' speech that Levi felt as though he were "hearing it for the first time"—it was, he said, "like the voice of God. For a moment I forget who I am and where I am."[4] Recalling Dante, Levi had a flash of disassociation, taking brief flight from his living hell. He noticed Pikolo listening intently to his recitation of Dante's lines. Levi sensed something profound had taken place in his fellow prisoner—that the spell of Dante's language had somehow transported his friend as well as himself. Perhaps, Levi thought, Jean understood that the passage from *Inferno* was meant "for all men who toil."[5] In Dante's poetry, recalled at the lowest possible moment of a human life, a common bond of humanity was forged.

When Levi and Pikolo arrived at the cafeteria, they had also reached the conclusion of Levi's discussion of the final lines of canto 26. Levi wanted to explain the meaning of Ulysses' last words in the poem, saying that it felt "vitally necessary and urgent" that Pikolo learn this message before it was too late, for tomorrow he and Pikolo "might be dead."[6] Their journey completed, Levi recalled Ulysses' fatal last line:

Until sea again closed—over us.[7]

Levi had arrived at a place of pure evil where all the joys of culture and laws of civilization had been suspended. He too could have lapsed into an animal state, doing everything possible to fend off death, even if it meant imperiling the lives of others. Yet, in the midst of his suffering, a powerful echo came to him—the sounds of beautiful words he had learned by heart. Dante's passage that "you were not made to live your lives as brutes, / but to be followers of worth and knowledge" resurfaced to connect him to Pikolo and to remind him of their humanity in an inhuman realm. Thus, in the horror of Auschwitz, the afterlife of the *Commedia* achieved one of its most astonishing rebirths.

———

Another poet for whom Dante became a matter of life or death was Levi's senior by two decades. Born to a Jewish family in Poland in 1891, Osip Mandelstam moved with his family to Saint Petersburg during one of the most tumultuous periods in the nation's history, as the country lurched from the Russian Revolution in 1917 to world war and finally Stalinist dictatorship. The situation for a poet like Mandelstam, who possessed a quasi-religious belief in the autonomy of poetry and the transformative power of art, could not have been worse. Like Levi and Dante, Mandelstam knew firsthand the lacerations of exile.

Yet his displacement was experienced not abroad but at home, as he was caught between the Scylla of creating art for political purposes and the Charybdis of defying a regime intent on stamping out artistic freedom. Mandelstam initially did neither, earning him censure from both the more collectivist-minded Soviet artists who were committed to promoting the new state and the courageously independent creators who openly defied the Communist regime and suffered the consequences, which more often than not were fatal. Mandelstam was like the composer Dmitri Shostakovich: physically unharmed but criticized by many, ostracized to the point where in the 1920s he could find few if any outlets to publish his work.

Banned from publishing his poetry and overcome with personal despair, Mandelstam could finally hold his peace no longer: in 1933, he wrote a poem characterizing Stalin as a sadistic killer who "rolls the executions on his tongue like berries."[8] The response was typically swift and categorical: Mandelstam was arrested and tortured—but not killed, thanks to the intercession of the prominent official Nikolai Bukarin, a lover of poetry. Instead, he was exiled to a remote village in the Ural Mountains. The persecutions continued after Mandelstam's return from exile in 1937, as he was once again arrested and consigned to a Soviet work camp and prison. He died in 1938 of typhoid fever in a transit camp; his corpse lay unburied for months and was eventually dumped into a mass grave.

Mandelstam's "Conversation about Dante" was written during this bleak final season of his life, from 1933 to 1935, but was not published until 1967. In it, the identification between him and Dante, as we saw with Levi, was intense and explicit: Mandelstam called Dante a "tortured and outcast" fellow sufferer.[9] Early in the essay, Mandelstam offered a T. S. Eliot–like gesture toward Dante's formal brilliance, describing him as a "master of the instruments of poetry."[10] Yet, as Wai Chee Dimock notes, echoing the Irish poet Seamus Heaney, Mandelstam's Dante was far different from Eliot's: whereas the latter saw Dante as a "stern and didactic" poet who stood atop the Latin-Italian literary tradition, Mandelstam was "gleefully a lost soul, gleefully unregenerate," who was more enticed by Dante's irruptive lyricism and "imperfect authority."[11]

As he was for so many writers, Dante for Mandelstam was all about language, the verbal surface of a *Commedia* that resonates across the centuries and the continents. He labeled Dante the vernacular poet par excellence, whose "creation is above all the entrance of the Italian language of his day onto the world stage."[12] The impression one has in reading "Conversation about Dante" is of how intensely Mandelstam *hears* Dante: the sound of his poetic voice, the reverberations of his hendecasyllables, and the echoes of his impassioned dialogues. Mandelstam wrote a book called *The Noise of Time* in 1925, a series of autobiographical sketches.[13] Evidence of his enthrallment with Dante's aurality fills Mandelstam's reading of *Inferno* 10: "A voice floats forward; it remains unclear to whom it belongs. . . . This voice—the first theme of Farinata [degli Uberti]—is the minor Dantean *arioso* of the suppliant type."[14] *Arioso*, a term associated with Bach, refers to vocal music that is more melodic than recitative but less formal than an aria. A musical passage or composition that mixes free recitative and metrical song, the *arioso* form is above all characterized by an emphasis on openness and freedom of association, which the Russian poet hears in the booming voice of the irrepressible Ghibelline general Farinata, when he surges out of his fiery tomb in *Inferno* 10 and announces to Dante: "O Tuscan, you who pass alive across / the fiery city with such seemly words" (*O Tosco che per la città del foco / vivo ten vai così parlando onesto*, 22–23). Just as Levi heard

Dante's words from *Inferno* 26 in Auschwitz ("Consider well the seed that gave you birth: / you were not made to live your lives as brutes, / but to be followers of worth and knowledge"), so too does the soothing balm of Dante's music emerge as a companion to Mandelstam in his journey through his personal hell.

So visceral was the call of Dante's verse for Mandelstam that he could feel the living presence of the *Commedia*, writing, "It is inconceivable to read Dante's cantos without directing them toward contemporaneity."[15] This perceived "nowness" of Dante and his impact on Mandelstam's life were perhaps most powerfully expressed in a hallucinatory passage toward the end of his essay: "If the halls of the Hermitage were suddenly to go mad, if the paintings of all the schools and the great masters were suddenly to break loose from the nails, and merge with one another, intermingle and fill the air of the rooms with a Futurist roar and an agitated frenzy of color, we would then have something resembling Dante's *Commedia*."[16]

———

A third figure who reached out to Dante in a moment of life-threatening adversity was Antonio Gramsci, the Italian statesman and theorist born in 1891, the same year as Mandelstam. A groundbreaking thinker with a range of interests outside of politics, Gramsci quickly rose through the ranks of left-wing circles, becoming head of the Partito Comunista Italiano (Italian Communist Party) and founding *Unità* (Unity), its official newspaper, in 1924. It was only a matter of time before so influential and capable an opposition leader as he would draw the scrutiny of the Fascist Party. In 1926, Mussolini's government instituted a series of emergency laws, ostensibly because of the attempted assassination of Mussolini by the Irish pacifist Violet

Gibson earlier that year. The police arrested Gramsci in open violation of his legislative immunity and deposited him in Rome's infamous Regina Coeli prison. The prosecutor at his trial remarked ominously that it was necessary to stop his "brain from functioning."[17] He received a sentence of twenty years. After eleven brutal years in jail, his health declined precipitously: his teeth fell out, he could not take in solid food, and his headaches were so bad that he beat his head against the wall in hopes of mitigating them.[18] After extensive medical treatment and shortly before his scheduled release from prison, Gramsci died in 1937 at age forty-six.

While in custody, Gramsci manage to write his influential *Quaderni del carcere* (Prison notebooks) between 1929 and 1935, more than thirty notebooks and three thousand pages of historical, cultural, and political analysis. Among the many topics he covered was his seminal concept of cultural hegemony, the notion that a ruling class manages to keep and extend its power by transforming their beliefs and values into dominant and unquestioned cultural norms. Gramsci's investment in Dante was lifelong, including during his prison years, and he was especially interested in *Inferno* 10, the canto of the heretical Epicureans, who included the Florentine patriarchs Farinata and Cavalcante de' Cavalcanti. In 1918, he wrote "The Blind Tiresias," an article that emphasized how throughout history those endowed with special powers, especially prophecy, are punished by society—often with the gruesome sentence of blinding, as in the case of the mythical Tiresias. Similarly, Gramsci writes, "Farinata and Cavalcante are punished for having wanted to see too far into the world beyond, and thus, because they have moved outside the bounds of Catholic discipline, they are punished by being deprived of all knowledge of the present."[19]

The energy put into this youthful reflection resurfaced in prison, where Gramsci wrote his most ambitious piece on Dante in his fifth notebook, "Canto 10 of the *Inferno*." His reading focused on the often-overlooked figure of Cavalcante de' Cavalcanti, father of Dante's *primo amico* and former mentor, Guido Cavalcanti. Gramsci says of the Tiresias-like Cavalcante that he "sees into the past and into the future, but he does not see the present."[20] Reviewing scholarship on the canto, Gramsci demolished a superficial reading by Vincenzo Morello. In opposition to the latter's reductive focus on such issues as whether Dante was Guelph or Ghibelline, Gramsci writes:

> In reality, Dante, as he himself says, "was a party unto himself"; he was basically an "intellectual," and his sectarianism and partisanship were more intellectual than political in the immediate sense. Besides, Dante's political position could only be determined by a most detailed analysis not only of all his writings but also of the political divisions of his time, which were very different from what they had been fifty years earlier. Morello is much too entangled in literary rhetoric to be able to have a realistic understanding of the political position of the men of the Middle Ages vis-à-vis the empire, the papacy, and their republican commune.[21]

Gramsci's allusion to *Paradiso* 17, where Dante is told by his ancestor Cacciaguida that he must become a "party of one," is crucial.[22] The advice comes as part of a moving sequence when Cacciaguida announces to Dante the protagonist what Dante the poet knows all too well: that he will be exiled, categorically and definitively, from the Florence he loves and will never see again.

"You shall leave everything you love most dearly:
this is the arrow that the bow of exile

shoots first. You are to know the bitter taste
of others' bread, how salt it is, and know
how hard a path it is for one who goes
descending and ascending others' stairs.
And what will be most hard for you to bear
will be the scheming, senseless company
that is to share your fall into this valley;
against you they will be insane, completely
ungrateful and profane; and yet, soon after,
not you but they will have their brows bloodred."

"Tu lascerai ogne cosa diletta
più caramente; e questo è quello strale
che l'arco de lo esilio pria saetta.
Tu proverai sì come sa di sale
lo pane altrui, e come è duro calle
lo scendere e 'l salir per l'altrui scale.
E quel che più ti graverà la spalle,
sarà la compagnia malvagia e scempia
con la qual tu cadrai in queste valle;
che tutta ingrata, tutta matta ed empia
si farà contr' a te; ma, poco appresso,
ella, non tu, n'avrà rossa la tempia." (Par. 17.55–66)

Dante's exile would indeed force him to struggle up the stairs
of strangers' homes, bear the wrath of malignant opponents,
and most memorably of all taste the "salty bread" of foreign
tables. It is impossible to know what Gramsci was thinking
as he languished in his cell and meditated on Dante's poem
while his body was slowly overcome by the maladies that would
cause his death. One senses, in reading his vigorous critique of
Morello's flat-footed political interpretation of Inferno 10, that
same passionate connection to Dante as a fellow sufferer and

humanizing presence that sustained Mandelstam and Levi. The *Commedia* became a mirror for their own superhuman struggles and, ultimately, a source of hope in an atmosphere of despair— yet despite the odds, and following Dante's example, they emerged heroic.

Chapter 9

Dante on Screen

CLOSE BY FLORENCE'S Arno, and amid the splendor of grand Renaissance museums like the Uffizi, it can be easy to overlook the Franco Zeffirelli Foundation. Devoted to the life and work of the city's native filmmaker and long-time set designer for New York's Metropolitan Opera, the museum contains a room dedicated to a movie that was never made: Zeffirelli's adaptation of Dante's *Inferno*. In this aptly named Sala Inferno, fifty-five sketches are exhibited as well as projected, in dramatic lighting, on the ceiling and walls. As an ominous soundtrack blares over the images, visitors might indeed feel as if they have passed through Dante's Gates of Hell with their injunction to abandon all hope.

The drawings and notes for this planned film take us inside Zeffirelli's lifelong investment in the *Commedia*. In his first sketch for *Inferno* 5, a detailed and fully colored rendering of a castle where Paolo stands by a door while Francesca looks down at him from a window, Zeffirelli carefully annotates the structure of the scene and its focus on, as he writes, "The Act of Love," "The Act of Damnation," "The Kiss—the Book That Closes," "Their Sex (Nude as They Are)," "The Death (Gianciotto Who Slays Them)," "The Eternal Pain—the Tears of Paolo," and "The Agony of Dante—Such That He Faints" (Figure 15).

FIGURE 15. Zeffirelli's drawing for *Inferno* 5, with notes. Courtesy of Fondazione Franco Zeffirelli, Firenze.

A subsequent panel reveals Zeffirelli's plans for creating a cinematic episode based on *Inferno* 5. He observes how "Dante witnesses the spectacle in bewilderment" (*Dante assiste sbalordito allo spettacolo*) and gestures toward the visuals of "orgies" (*orgie*) and "flesh" (*la carne*) that will punctuate his representation of the sexual dramas surrounding the "nude and bloodied" (*nudi e insanguinati*) Paolo and Francesca. The panel even includes the citation of actual verses from Dante's famous canto, with its haunting concluding line of an overwhelmed Dante saying, "I fell as a dead body falls" (*caddi come corpo morto cade, Inf.* 5.142).

A final drawing from the canto functions as a closeup: the lovers, naked and wrapped in each other's arms, are observed by Dante and Virgil who view the scene from the same perspective as we the audience (Figure 16). Dante and his guide bear sol-

FIGURE 16. Second drawing by Zeffirelli of *Inferno* 5. Courtesy of Fondazione Franco Zeffirelli, Firenze.

emn witness to the lovers' tragic story, distilled into the image of their heated embrace. In Zeffirelli's deeply erotic interpretation of Dante's original canto, which often obscures its sexual content—leading one scholar to describe how "Dante desexualizes lust"—there is something voyeuristic in Dante's and Virgil's gaze, with their faces and eyes hidden from us.[1] They— and we the audience—are witnessing the most intimate moment in Paolo and Francesca's story, the one that will seal their love but also cost them their lives. Such sketches make one wonder what a Zeffirelli adaptation of the *Commedia* as a whole might have been like: closely aligned with Dante's original text, filled with narrative drama and intensity, and charged with a highly emotional and evocative atmosphere that updated

Dante's medieval horizon of concerns to our own more graphic notions of sexuality.

It is not surprising that Zeffirelli, who spent part of his childhood in Florence's Hospital of the Innocents, the fabled home for abandoned children created in the Renaissance, was fascinated by this epic poem from his city's most famous literary son. Indeed, the history of Italian cinema, or at least the history of the nation's narrative cinema, actually *begins* with Dante. *L'Inferno* from 1911, directed by Francesco Bertolini, Giuseppe de Liguoro, and Adolfo Padovan, was the first feature-length film made in Italy. It exhibits a level of sophistication and artistic flair that in retrospect is astounding. The depictions of hell are based on Gustave Doré's iconic illustrations, lending the film a highly stylized, gothic visual beauty, and the special effects are cutting-edge, including flashbacks, superimposition of images, and double exposures.[2] The prestige of Dante's *Commedia* lent an air of legitimacy to the fledgling medium of film, which frequently turned to the *Sommo Poeta* in its early years: between 1908 and 1911, eleven films inspired by either the *Commedia*, Dante's life, or figures from his poem premiered in Italy.[3]

L'Inferno by Bertolini, de Liguoro, and Padovan follows Dante's text fairly closely. It opens with Dante prevented from ascending the hill of salvation by three beasts representing Avarice, Pride, and Lust, at which point Beatrice descends from her heavenly perch to petition Virgil to serve as Dante's guide through hell and its nine circles. Many of the notorious scenes of Dantesque *contrapasso*, counter-penalty, are in full effect, as a sower of discord carries his own severed head, and the familiar monsters—Geryon, the half-man and half-beast representing fraud, and Cerberus, the three-headed hound of hell—are also on view. With its high production values and sophisticated content, the film became a precursor of historical epics like Giovanni Pastrone's *Cabiria* (1914). To this day, it is considered a masterpiece of the silent screen.[4]

The *Commedia* also influenced cinematic work in the world's leading center for film production, Hollywood. Several films based on Dante's ill-fated Francesca from *Inferno* 5 appeared on the American silent screen, and in the age of sound Harry Lachman's *Dante's Inferno* from 1935 offered a modern morality tale that followed the life of ruthless Jim Carter (played by Spencer Tracy), who inherits a fairground concession called "Dante's Inferno" and then causes it to collapse so that he can construct a palace of sin and debauchery in its place.[5] Though relatively few American films since have been straightforward adaptations of the *Commedia*, references and allusions to Dante's epic have appeared in a wealth of major movies, including those directed by Francis Ford Coppola, Tim Burton, David Lynch, Adrian Lyne, and especially Martin Scorsese.[6] A recent study by Catherine O'Brien, *Martin Scorsese's Divine Comedy: Movies and Religion* (2018), likens the filmmaker's oeuvre to a cinematic *Commedia* by exploring religion in Scorsese's films and connecting his treatment of issues of sin and salvation to wider debates about eschatology and the afterlife.[7]

Dante's influence in European auteur cinema has also been pronounced. These directors found in Dante a kindred spirit: his writing was as personal and uncompromising as their films aspired to be. Just as Dante's "signature" is everywhere in his poetry—much of his creative work bore the stamp of palinode, the medieval rhetorical trope of self-revision[8]—so too did auteur directors wish to make a "pen" of their cameras and metaphorically create their films in highly individual and idiosyncratic styles.[9] In a sense, auteur cinema synthesized two major historical approaches to Dante's work: first, they celebrated the Romantic idea of Dante as a heroic artist who transcended the politics of his age to create his great poem, much like Federico Fellini's character Guido Anselmi in *8½* (1963), the director experiencing a midlife crisis who seeks to escape the tether, both literal and figurative, of an executive who pulls his floating body down to earth while he dreams. Second, auteurs adopted High Modernist practices of aesthetic difficulty and formal innovation in translating scenes and motifs from the *Commedia* into highly wrought symbolic elements in their films.

Dantesque themes permeate Fellini's auteurist masterpiece *La dolce vita* (1960), which features a modern-day pilgrim, Marcello, in search of a guide through Roman high society.[10] The film ends with Marcello—after "having lost his way" just as Dante had at the beginning of *Inferno* (*ché la via diretta era smaritta, Inf.* 1.3)—reunited with his Beatrice-like figure, the young Paola, an innocent waitress whose purity and selfless concern for Marcello contrasts with his other hedonistic and empty relations. In the haunting conclusion, a beached tuna stares at Marcello and his debauched friends, neutrally but somehow accusingly ("How he looks at us!" one of Marcello's entourage exclaims). Meanwhile, Paola gazes on, beckoning Marcello to leave his spiritual squalor and join her on a presumably better path. But there is no such *Commedia*-like hope of salvation in Marcello's fallen world: he cynically waves her away and returns to his licentious group.

Another major auteur work to rely on the poetry of the *Commedia* was Michelangelo Antonioni's *Deserto rosso* (Red desert, 1964), the final film in the groundbreaking tetralogy that included *L'avventura* (1960), *La notte* (1961), and *L'eclisse* (1962). Antonioni's first color film, *Red Desert* succeeds in transforming color into a "character," giving it qualities and characteristics as vivid as those of the people who inhabit this dystopian world of ecological degradation and emotional alienation in Ravenna, Dante's final place of rest. An example of what Pier Paolo Pasolini called the "cinema of poetry," *Red Desert* contains what one scholar describes as "a sophisticated chain of Dantean allusions," including a visit by the Ulysses-like wanderer Corrado to the protagonist Giuliana's shop on Via Alighieri as well as an encounter between Giuliana and a fruit vendor who resembles Dante's Infernal ferryman, Charon.[11]

Perhaps the most sustained cinematic engagement with the *Commedia* comes in a work that cites it openly: Jean-Luc Godard's *Le mépris* (Contempt, 1963). We saw earlier how Mary Shelley's response to Dante's canto of Ulysses represented a typically Romantic reading that emphasized her protagonist Victor Frankenstein's heroic aspirations. That same scene from Dante would return, with different effects, in *Contempt*, an adaptation of Alberto Moravia's *Il disprezzo* (Contempt, 1954). The film tells the story of the French screenwriter Paul Javal, a self-absorbed intellectual who is married to the more down-to-earth Camille (played by the international sex symbol Brigitte Bardot). Javal is called to Cinecittà in Rome to write a modern-day adaptation of the *Odyssey* that is to be directed by the legendary German auteur Fritz Lang (played by himself) and produced by the corrupt and crass American producer Jeremiah Prokosch (played with malicious glee by Jack Palance).

Early in the film, the team meets in a screening room to view rushes and discuss the process of adaptation. Allusions to dramatic scenes in Homer's epic source, with the gods represented by painted statues, are constantly undermined by references to the artificial off-screen world of filmmaking. Lang's still-life view of Minerva is juxtaposed with shots of the projectionist; a 180-degree pan of Ulysses is countered by the gaze of his modern rewriter, Javal; and Minerva's monumental beauty and immobile elegance are swarmed by the clapperboard and other stage props. Godard's parodic attitude toward adaptation reaches its apotheosis in the linking of the inscription "Odysseus" to "Jeremiah Prokosch Productions."

Then Dante comes in. After the appearance of a bust of Homer, the frivolous irreverence of Godard's poetic adaptation switches gears to a more poignant and delicate register. The marble statues give way to human actors, and the figure of Ulysses stringing his bow is followed by the intonation of verses that, though seemingly Homeric in their literary theme and accompanying visual content, actually derive from the *Commedia*: "O my brothers, who braved 100,000 perils to reach the west, choose not to deny experience of the unpeopled world." This citation from *Inferno* 26 sets in motion a series of intense intertextual and intermedial exchanges that contrast ancient epic and medieval literature to the much younger medium of film. The scene is also an exercise in verbal translation, as Homer's original is recast into Dante's Italian and then into Lang's German, Javal's French, and Prokosch's English. Godard's multilingual, Babel-like linguistic refraction of Dante's Tuscan lines reveals the multinational, corporate nature of this large-scale cinematic production, the iconoclastic Godard's first and last big-budget work.[12]

As his marriage to Camille steadily unravels, Javal sees in Ulysses' plight a mirror of his own. He says to Lang that Ulysses actually tarried as long as possible in order to avoid returning to Ithaca, his unfaithful wife, and his unhappy marital life. Whereas in Dante Ulysses suffers from an intellectual restlessness that drives him from the very home whose spirit defined him in the ancient source, in Godard Ulysses is the victim of feminine wiles and—more poignantly with respect to Homer—his inability to control his domestic realm and fulfill the duties of patriarchy. And whereas in Dante's *Inferno* Ulysses remains a figure of extreme rhetorical brilliance (despite his misguided use of his talents and the punishment it brings about), in Godard's *Contempt* Ulysses—like the character Javal himself—is a petulant, petty, and ineffective presence. Lang's character brilliantly sums up Paul's ersatz Homeric adaptation: "Ulysses in Homer is a simple, robust, and clever man. You cannot transform him into a modern-day neurotic."

Another powerful auteur response to the *Commedia* came from the Polish film director Krzystof Kieślowski. A deeply literary filmmaker, Kieślowski directed the trilogy *Blue, White,* and *Red* (1993–94), whose tripartite structure is said to have been loosely based on Dante's three-canticle division in *The Divine Comedy*.[13] After finishing the Three Colors trilogy, Kieślowski planned to create a new trilogy that would be more directly inspired by Dante's *Commedia*, but he died in 1996, two years after the release of *Red*. The German director Tom Tykwer eventually shot the film *Heaven* in 2002, using Kieślowski's original screenplay, and in 2005, the Bosnian director Danis Tanović directed *Hell* based on Kieślowski's screenplay sketches, which had been completed by Krzystof Piesiewicz, Kieślowski's screenwriter. Kieślowski's planned *Purgatory* has never been produced.

Kieślowski's most direct and sustained engagement with Dante was in his critically acclaimed *The Double Life of Veronica* (1991), one of few films to quote from Dante's epic at length. It tells the story of two identical women, the French Véronique and the Polish Weronika, born on the same day and raised primarily by their fathers. They never actually meet except for a fleeting and chance encounter in Kraków when the French Véronique, passing through the city as a tourist, accidentally photographs her Polish doppelgänger. The first half of the film follows the life of Weronica, who devotes herself to a singing career at the expense of her fragile health—she actually dies during a performance halfway through the film. The second half charts the fate of Véronique, who gives up singing to protect her health and begins to receive what seem to be messages from her deceased metaphysical twin.

In the pivotal scene where Weronika suffers a fatal heart attack, she performs before a packed audience in Kraków and sings the beautiful opening of *Paradiso* 2 in its original Tuscan:

O you who are within your little bark,
eager to listen, following behind
my ship that, singing, crosses to deep seas,
turn back to see your shores again: do not
attempt to sail the seas I sail; you may,
by losing sight of me, be left astray.
The waves I take were never sailed before;
Minerva breathes, Apollo pilots me,
and the nine Muses show to me the Bears.

O voi che siete in piccioletta barca,
desiderosi d'ascoltar, seguiti
dietro al mio legno che cantando varca,
tornate a riveder li vostri liti:
non vi mettete in pelago, ché forse,
perdendo me, rimarreste smarriti.
L'acqua ch'io prendo già mai non si corse;
Minerva spira, e conducemi Appollo,
e nove Muse mi dimostran l'Orse. (1–9)

The words were set to music by Zbigniew Preisner, the distinguished Polish composer and Kieślowski's longtime collaborator who has also contributed to the soundtracks of films by such noted directors as Terence Malick and Paolo Sorrentino. Kieślowski's reference to Dante suggests his strong understanding of the original text, for Dante's address to the reader in *Paradiso* 2 recalls two key moments in the *Commedia* that are relevant to Weronika's fatal song: the entrance into the "dark wood" (*selva oscura*) in *Inferno* 1 and the shipwreck, actual and allegorical, of Ulysses in *Inferno* 26. Like Dante the pilgrim who finds himself in a dark wood "after having lost the right path," so too does Dante in *Paradiso* 2 warn readers not to lose sight of him lest they "be left astray" (*rimarreste smarriti*). The reader is asked to follow Dante humbly, "in a little bark" (*in piccioletta barca*) with none of the intellectual hubris that led Ulysses and his men on a "mad journey" (*folle volo*) in their shipwreck in *Inferno* 26. The Polish Weronika is about to cross that allegorical line suggested by Dante's verses: despite her poor health, she decides to pursue her dream of a high-profile singing career, when her frail health is clearly incapable of sustaining the exertions this path will entail. Her French double, Véronique, takes the more prudent route, anchoring the little bark (*piccioletta barca*) of her career not in the grand dreams of her exuberant Polish other but rather in the more humble life of a music school teacher. Weronika decides to risk the open sea of the artist's life and, tragically, her singing only briefly "crosses to deep seas."

It is a tragic irony of the auteur tradition that two directors exquisitely poised to take on full adaptations of Dante, Franco Zeffirelli and Krzysztof Kieślowski, were never able to make their cinematic versions of the *Commedia* a reality. Indeed, such an adaptation remains something of a white whale in the film industry—a project often discussed and even planned, yet to date still unrealized. One commentator went so far as to pen the provocative piece "Hollywood! Adapt This: Dante Alighieri's *The*

Divine Comedy," staking out a claim for the visual and thematic splendor of Dante's poem before wistfully concluding, "there's simply no enthusiasm [in Hollywood] for an expensive and unproven property [like Dante's *Commedia*], even if that property takes audiences through a journey not just through the fires of Hell itself, but into redemption and beyond. Stories like this just aren't seen as profitable in the material world, even if they'd work wonders for the spiritual one."[14] Another put it more starkly, invoking the video game *Inferno* and its beefed-up hero, Dante: "The market for religious allegory-based franchise isn't quite as big as the one for action superheroes who fight their way through hell in order to save their loves."[15] The sentiments are ones that might have drawn a knowing nod from Dante himself, a writer who devoted enormous amounts of energy to denouncing materialism and love of money, especially in his hyper-mercantile native Florence and papal Rome, "where—every day—Christ is both sold and bought" (*là dove Cristo tutto dì si merca, Par.* 17.51). So far the attempts made in translating Dante's *poema* to the screen remain tentative and artisanal, with no wide diffusion.[16] So the *Commedia* awaits a filmmaker, an heir of Zeffirelli and Kieślowski—perhaps a Scorsese, Spielberg, or Campion—willing to rise to Dante's epic challenge.

Chapter 10

Trigger Warnings and Papal Blessings

IN 2012, ABOUT five hundred years after the Spanish Inquisition had sought to repress passages in the *Commedia* that were deemed unacceptable, the Italian human rights advocacy group Gherush92 called for the removal of Dante's epic from school curricula and university syllabi. According to the organization's president, Valentina Sereni, the *Commedia* "represents Islam as a heresy and Mohammed as a schismatic and refers to Jews as greedy, scheming moneylenders and traitors. . . . The Prophet Mohammed was subjected to a horrific punishment—his body was split from end to end so that his entrails dangled out, an image that offends Islamic culture."[1] Sereni added, "We do not advocate censorship or the burning of books, but we would like it acknowledged, clearly and unambiguously, that in the Divine Comedy there is racist, Islamophobic and anti-Semitic content. Art cannot be above criticism."[2] Drawing a parallel between Dante's inflammatory remarks about other religions and actual persecutions inflicted by fascist regimes in the twentieth century, the Gherush92 manifesto concluded:

It is a scandal that children, and in particular Jewish and Islamic youth, are forced to study racist works like *The Divine Comedy*, which under the cover of art hides all manner of nefariousness. Antisemitism, Islamophobia, Antigypsism, and racism should be fought against as we seek to ally ourselves with historic victims of racism now exposed by themes and arguments like cultural diversity.[3]

The proposed ban had no effect, and the *Commedia* remains probably the most studied book in Italy, where Dante continues to be revered as the *Sommo Poeta* whose statues and monuments fill the nation's public spaces.[4] Support was scant even among groups with whom Gherush92 sought to ally itself against the *Commedia*: Italian cultural associations and gay rights groups joined in defending Dante against such accusations, accusing Gherush92 of "an excess of political correctness."[5]

Yet the group's efforts are not unique. The *Commedia* has been banned from Texas state prisons[6] as well as from the entire nation of Kuwait.[7] Such politically charged responses should come as no surprise, since Dante's work has always served as a rallying cry for the both the left and the right. As we have seen, during Dante's Romantic resurgence in nineteenth-century Britain, he became the darling of politically radical poets like Byron and Shelley, while the more conservative Wordsworth derided his work in part because of his aversion to the ideological views of his progressive-minded contemporaries. Italy, understandably, has been the site for the ongoing political negotiation of Dante's legacy for centuries.[8] When the nation was finally unified in 1861, many hailed Dante as a father of the country, especially because of his efforts on behalf of the Tuscan vernacular, which became the nation's official language. In 1865, when Florence was named the capital, a nineteen-foot-high cenotaph was erected to Dante in Piazza Santa Croce to mark the occasion, with thousands attending the inauguration of the statue amid a host of musical and literary celebrations. Specially commissioned poems were read in Dante's honor, as was a letter from Victor Hugo, whose stirring words essentially equated Italy's birth with Dante's name, with the renowned French poet's enthusiasm evident in his all-caps spelling:

> Italy, it seems to me, desires to be born on the same day as DANTE. This nation wishes to bear the same date as that man. Italy, in fact incarnates herself in DANTE ALIGHIERI. Like him she is valiant, pensive, proud, magnanimous, prepared for battle, prepared for thought. Like him she blends in a profound synthesis, poetry and philosophy. Like him she is determined to have liberty. He has, like her, the grandeur which he puts into life, and the beauty which he puts into his works. Italy and DANTE are commingled in a mutual kind of interpenetration which makes them one; they shine out each in the other. She is august as he is illustrious. They have the same heart, the same will, the same destiny. She resembles him by that mighty latent power which DANTE and Italy have had in adversity. She is a Queen—he genius. Like him she has been prescribed; like him she is crowned.[9]

Political passion for Dante can also take a more ominous turn. As they did for so many other cultural figures—including the bookish and decidedly non-soldierly Petrarch[10]—Italian Fascists seized on Dante's cult of the Roman Empire and planned to erect the Danteum, an unbuilt monument approved by Mussolini that was to rise in the Forum and extol the regime's militarist values.[11] The expropriation of Dante's meaning in the name of nationalist fervor continues to the present: around the time of this writing, Gennaro Sangiuliano, the Italian culture minister, called Dante "the founder of right-wing thinking in our country" (*il fondatore del pensiero di destra italiano*), a specious claim that many have hotly contested.[12]

A less-known chapter in the history of politicized responses to the *Commedia* is that the work has been subject to "trigger warnings," statements cautioning that a book's content may be disturbing or upsetting or even have potentially traumatic effects on its readers. The website Book Trigger Warnings, whose mission is "to create a central place for readers to visit and check for specific triggers, tropes, representation and/or controversies that may factor into their decision to pick up a specific book," lists the following triggers for Dante's *Inferno*: "bestiality," "blood," "gore," "hornet/wasp attacks," "torture," and "violence (graphic)."[13]

While it may strain the imagination to connect warnings as diverse as Vernani's denunciation of Dante as the "devil's vessel" in 1327 and the trigger of "hornet/wasp attacks" in 2022, the history of Dante's censorship over the past seven hundred years reveals key common characteristics. First, Dante's offended readers belong to a plurality of religious groups and political persuasions, with no single faith or ideology holding sway. The *Commedia* has been attacked by Christians and non-Christians, conservatives and liberals alike.[14] For example, the Spanish Inquisition purged Dante's epic for not being "pure" enough and for swerving from Church dogma, while Gherush92 sought to remove the *Commedia* from Italian classrooms because it adopted positions disrespectful of other religions—in other words, because it was too typically Christian and Eurocentric in its orientations. As the plurality and diversity of the above interpretations show, Dante's *Commedia* has been "all things to all men" (1 Corinthians 9:22), with no predictive patterns to the responses.

Despite the media noise generated by such provocative calls to ban or censure the *Commedia*, its place in the global canon and public imaginary has never seemed as secure and lofty as the present day. In 2018, an article in the *Irish Times* proclaimed Dante's *Commedia* "the greatest single work of Western literature," and popular actors like Roberto Benigni have thrilled audiences worldwide with public performances of Dante's verse.[15] The seven hundredth anniversary of Dante's death in 2021 set off a wave of events celebrating Dante's legacy, including the initiative "100 Days of Dante," the world's largest Dante reading group, which produced short, accessible videos by scholars and experts to guide aficionados through the *Commedia*. In testament to the diversity of responses it has inspired, Dante's afterlife now includes the hashtag #100daysofdante.

Perhaps the greatest indicator of how Dante's *Commedia* has been transformed from the bane of the Spanish Inquisitors to the darling of religious thinkers throughout the world is its reception by a group that Dante represented with venomous ink: the popes. Astonishingly, the *Commedia*, chock-full of antipapal sentiment, has become a revered text in the Vatican. Pope Benedict XV's "In Praeclara Summorum" (Among the many celebrated) stands out as a key moment in this transition. In 1921, the six hundredth anniversary of Dante's death, this papal encyclical—addressed "to professors and students of literature and learning in the Catholic world"—announced the "intimate union of Dante with this Chair of Peter" and declared that "the praises showered on that distinguished name [Dante] necessarily redound in no small measure to the honour of the Catholic Church."[16] The pope's rhetorical gesture of saying that the praise of one (Dante) signaled the praise of another (the Catholic Church) recalls Dante's biographies in *Paradiso* of Saint Francis by the Dominican Aquinas and Saint

Dominic by the Franciscan Bonaventure. As the character Aquinas notes, "in praising either prince one praises both: / the labors of the two were toward one goal" (*si dice l'un pregiando, qual ch'om prende, / perch' ad un fine fur l'opere sue, Par.* 11.41–42). Benedict showed himself to be a careful reader of Dante, as he alludes directly to the dramatic scene in *Paradiso* 25 when Dante speaks of the labors cost him by the writing of his poem, highlighting Dante's "desire of being crowned poet at the very font where he had received Baptism," Florence's Baptistery of San Giovanni. In Benedict's view, the combination of Dante's secular learning and the energies that went into writing the *Commedia* had for "its true aim the glorification of the justice and providence of God who rules the world through time and all eternity and punishes and rewards the actions of individuals and human society." Benedict even gestures toward a dangerous subject, the Church's dominion in earthly affairs—the same subject that motivated Vernani's polemic against Dante's *De monarchia*—and expresses his agreement with Dante's "great reverence for the authority of the Catholic Church, the account in which he holds the power of the Roman Pontiff as the base of every law and institution of that Church." In sum, Benedict concludes, Dante was "the most eloquent singer of the Christian idea. The more profit you draw from study of him the higher will be your culture, irradiated by the splendours of truth, and the stronger and more spontaneous your devotion to the Catholic Faith."

Pope Paul VI was equally celebratory, writing on the seven hundredth anniversary of Dante's birth in his apostolic letter "Altissimi Cantus" (The highest songs) from 1966. He called Dante "the lord of the sublime song," while acknowledging him as author of "fertile poetry" and the "father of the Italian language."[17] Paul situated Dante among the "Christian poets," a group including Prudentius and Saint Ambrose, and announced that the Vatican would create a chair in Dante Studies at the Catholic University of the Sacred Heart in Milan. Most astonishing of all, Paul tolerated Dante's anti-papal rhetoric:

> Nor do we regret the fact that the voice of Dante lashed out severely against more than one Roman Pontiff, and had harsh reproofs for ecclesiastical institutions and for persons who were representatives and ministers of the Church. We do not hide this moment of his spirit and this aspect of his work, knowing well what caused this bitterness of soul, even his own beloved city of Florence and Italy itself, were not spared such harsh reprimands; one can concede indulgence in regard to his art and political passion, that the office of judge and corrector was taken over by him, especially before pitiable circumstances, and yet, such fiery attitudes never weakened his firm Catholic faith and his filial affection for Holy Church.

In his acceptance of Dante's ad hominem attacks on specific popes, Paul VI astutely understood that Dante never questioned the supremacy of the papacy per se. Just as he rebuked many individual kings and emperors while remaining steadfastly committed to the offices of monarchy and empire, so too, as Paul writes, Dante "acknowledged and venerated in the Roman Pontiff the Vicar of Christ on earth." Nor does Paul call out Dante for what many of his Christian confreres had censured: his love of pagan antiquity. Invoking the encyclopedic breadth of the *Commedia*, Paul writes that it contains, inter alia, "Greek logos, Roman civility, and, in synthesis, the dogmas, precepts and laws of Christianity in the elaboration of the Fathers and Doctors of the Church."

A key component of Paul's reading of Dante was his sensitivity to Dante's love for the mystic tradition. He describes the

Commedia as a work in the spirit of Bonaventure's *The Mind's Journey to God*, "from darkness of inexorable reprobation, to the tears of purifying expiation, and, from step to step, from brightness to brightness." He then highlights Dante's devotion to the beloved queen of the mystics, the Virgin Mary: "Indeed, for the Florentine Poet, Mary [represents] 'il nome del bel fior ch'io sempre invoco e mane e sera,' [the name of the beautiful flower which I invoke morning and evening, *Par.* 23.88–89] . . . she is the dispenser of graces, she is the shining portal of Heaven who, bridging the distance between Christ and creatures, permits access to Christ and to the beatitude of eternal Truth." He also praises the philosophical side of Dante and his adherence to the intellectual giants of the Church, especially Thomas Aquinas. He defends Dante's humanism, defining it as "well opposed to current mystics-ascetics [who] seem to point to contempt for the world as an ideal. In Dante all human values (intellectual, moral, emotional, cultural, civil) are recognized and exalted. What is very important to understand is that this truth is appreciated and given honor by Dante as he comes to plumb the depths of the divine." Weighing in on the eternal debate over whether Dante was principally a poet or theologian, Paul took a synthetic view: "Both these titles [poet and theologian] are right and just. Although a theologian, Dante is in no way restrained from being a poet, on the contrary, he is rather to be proclaimed the 'lord of sublime song' as well as a theologian of eminent thought." Gesturing toward the fusion of the secular and the sacred in the *Commedia*, he concludes that Dante's poetry is "a dazzling star to which one turns to look and to ask the way to the good road, which is often impeded by a dark wood, to that which Dante points out to us, his 'dilettoso monte / ch'è principio e cagion di tutta gioia'" (the mountain of delight / the origin and cause of every joy, *Inf.* 1.77–78).

Not surprisingly, the pontiff at the time of this book's writing, Pope Francis—who took the name of one of Dante's most beloved spiritual figures, Saint Francis of Assisi—has also had much to say about the *Commedia*. In his apostolic letter "Candor Lucis Aeternae" (The splendor of eternal light), written on the seven hundredth anniversary of Dante's death in 2021, Francis returned to Paul VI's celebration of Dante as mystic, referencing Saint Bernard's celebration of the Incarnation in *Paradiso* 33:

> "Within thy womb rekindled was the love,
> By heat of which in the eternal peace
> After such wise this flower has germinated."

> *"Nel ventre tuo si raccese l'amore,*
> *per lo cui caldo ne l'etterna pace*
> *così è germinato questo fiore." (Par.* 33.7–9)[18]

Francis acknowledged his "wish to join my Predecessors who honoured and extolled the poet Dante, particularly on the anniversaries of his birth or death, and to propose him anew for the consideration of the Church, the great body of the faithful, literary scholars, theologians and artists." This sense of a papal tradition in interpreting and praising Dante is noteworthy considering the initial resistance within the Vatican to Dante's poem because of its consistently antagonistic attitude toward certain individual popes. Francis even summarized the representations of Dante by earlier popes, including Benedict XV, Leo XIII, Saint Pius X, and Saint Paul VI. He was thus the first pope to offer a literary history of papal responses to the *Commedia*, which suggests that his own contribution was shaped by the thoughts and opinions of earlier pontiffs.[19]

Francis's encomium of Dante is marked by his willingness to explore the relevance of the *Commedia* to the world today.

Emphasizing the link between past and present when reading Dante, Francis spoke of his desire "to consider the life and work of the great poet and examine its 'resonance' with our own experience," its "perennial timeliness." He described Dante's autobiography, focusing on his exile as a "paradigm of the human condition, viewed as a journey—spiritual and physical—that continues until it reaches its goal." Ultimately, Francis writes, that sense of permanent dislocation and displacement led to Dante's religious vocation, inspiring his role as the "prophet of a new humanity that thirsts for peace and happiness."

Echoing Paul VI, Francis also underscored Dante's connection to the Virgin Mary, quoting the scene toward the end of *Paradiso* 33 when the poet depicts the eternal Word made flesh in the womb of Mary:

> Within the deep and luminous subsistence
> Of the High Light appeared to me three circles
> Of threefold colour and of one dimension . . .
> That circulation, which being thus conceived
> Appeared in thee as a reflected light
> When somewhat contemplated by mine eyes
> Within itself, of its own very colour
> Seemed to me painted with our effigy.

> *Ne la profonda e chiara sussistenza*
> *de l'alto lume parvermi tre giri*
> *di tre colori e d'una contenenza . . .*
> *Quella circulazion che sì concetta*
> *pareva in te come lume reflesso,*
> *da li occhi miei alquanto circunspetta,*
> *dentro da sé, del suo colore stesso,*
> *mi parve pinta de la nostra effige.* (*Par.* 33.115–17, 127–31)

In the spirit of what he calls Dante's "splendid treatise of Mariology," Francis references the "three women of the *Comedy*," Beatrice, Saint Lucy, and the Virgin Mary, before moving to a discussion of his namesake, Saint Francis. The pope emphasizes how Dante and Saint Francis had much in common, including their devotion to the vernacular: Francis's *Cantico delle creature* (Canticle of the creatures, 1224) was one of the first dialect poems in all of Italian literature, anticipating Dante's legendary efforts in this domain. Pope Francis also underscored Dante and Saint Francis's mutual "sensitivity to the beauty and worth of creation as the reflection and imprint of its Creator." In speaking so passionately about Dante's connection to Saint Francis, the pope seems to be forging his own autobiographical connection to the *Commedia*. His personal investment in Dante's vision comes through toward the conclusion of the encyclical, when he beseeches his readers, at a juncture in history "overclouded by situations of profound inhumanity and a lack of confidence and prospects for the future," to heed Dante's message more than ever. Dante, Francis writes, was a "prophet of hope" who ended his *Commedia* with the most joyful conclusion to an epic ever written: a journey to God and a vision of the "Love which moves the sun and the other stars" (*Par.* 33.145).

As we allow Dante's beautiful closing words from *Paradiso* to resonate and as we reflect on the enduring life of Dante's *Commedia* in culture—as both a great religious book and a secular text of incalculable influence—it seems fitting to wonder about the faith of Dante himself. What were the spiritual issues and concerns, the beliefs and doubts, and the religious passions that inspired his great poem? Peter Hawkins answers these questions eloquently:

> . . . one might say that [Dante's] faith, at least as we can discern it in his writing, was like that of most religious people—a

mixture of received tradition and personal idiosyncrasy. He lived at a time of religious fervor but also of turmoil and crisis. Given his evangelical impulses, it was important for him to affirm the central teachings of Catholic Christianity: belief in the Triune God, the Incarnation of Christ, and the authority of the Scriptures, as well a conversion of heart, soul, mind, and strength. At the same time, he made orthodox faith very much his own. He took liberties when he wanted to, or when the dictates of his imagination "called" him to do so. Because his experience of Christ came to him most powerfully through the person of Mary and the figure of Beatrice, he affirmed the Incarnation in woman's flesh. His poem became "scripture" of his gospel, and over the course of the *Commedia* he so transfigured the human smile that it took on all the power of the sign of the cross. Whether inspired by the nine Muses or the Holy Spirit (or some combination of the two), Dante gave us a new account of everything old.[20]

Hawkins's observation points to the mix of scriptural tradition and personal spirituality in Dante's religious vision, while also reminding us of the unresolvable tensions in Dante's work and the manifold ways it has been read throughout history. Inveterate realist for some, divinely inspired prophet for others, Dante sang of multiple, often competing worlds with one unified creative voice, moving between elements as opposed as Christian spiritual salvation and Roman imperial rule, or as divided as his heartbreaking love of Florence and his Savonarola-like denunciation of the greed and corruption of the *fiorentini*—described acidly by Brunetto Latini as "that malicious, that ungrateful people" (*quello ingrato popolo maligno*, *Inf.* 15.61). Ultimately, we, his readers, choose to inhabit those aspects of Dante that draw us in the most, at times leading us to defend our Dantesque turf

against other interpretations with the zeal of the true believer
and the scholarly rigor of the *dantista*.[21] But in the end, all of us
contribute to the same ever-expanding and ever-diverse multi-
plicity of possible responses that the *Commedia* manages to
engender. Since we began with Shelley's description of Dantesque poetry as a "fountain forever overflowing with the waters
of wisdom and delight," it seems fitting to end in a similar place.
As Shelley wrote in his "A Defence of Poetry," after one person
and one age has exhausted all the "divine effluence" of a great
poem, another and yet another succeeds, "the source of an unforeseen and an unconceived delight."

Dante said as much. Not long before *The Divine Comedy*'s
concluding image of the sun and stars held together by cosmic
love, the character Dante meets the father of humanity, biblical
Adam, who offers him the following advice:

> "That man should speak at all is nature's act,
> but how you speak—in this tongue or in that—
> she leaves to you and to your preference."

> *"Opera naturale è ch'uom favella;*
> *ma così o così, natura lascia*
> *poi fare a voi secondo che v'abbella." (Par. 26.130–32)*

The key word here is in the Tuscan original: *abbellare*, to find
pleasure or, closer to the word's root, to seek the beautiful
(*bello*). Dante wrote this verse after decades of upheaval and
duress that had altered almost every detail of his personal life.
Yet from the mouth of the Bible's first human to the ears of the
character Dante and finally the eyes of his readers, one thing
remained a constant to him: the belief that great literature
brings a particular joy, one powerful enough to outdistance
what Dante called the arrow of exile. Reading the *Commedia*

certainly requires its share of intellectual labor and metaphysical sweat, but ultimately anyone cast into its orbit does well to
heed Adam's view. In the spirit of his words, this book has tried
to tell the story of those who, following their pleasure and in
some cases their pain, have dared to take Dante's path from the
dark wood to the stars.

Acknowledgments

This book was in many ways born in the classroom, where for decades now I have been blessed to study and then teach Dante in the most inspiring of settings. Way back in the 1990s, John Freccero first opened my eyes to the possibilities of Dante studies in my Master's program at NYU, and afterward Giuseppe Mazzotta, my dissertation adviser, guided me through the Ph.D. program at Yale with his astonishing mix of erudition and creativity in interpreting Dante. Most consequential of all has been my time at Bard, where since 2002, I have had the privilege of teaching Dante on a regular basis. Perhaps more than anything, this book is about how Dante established a breathtakingly original work whose mysteries and meanings each generation tries to discover in ways that are relevant to its world. For me, that magical space where Dante is brought to life in the present tense has been in class with my Bard students—to all of them, thank you.

The gestation period for this book has been a long one, and I am deeply indebted to my entire team at Princeton University Press for their patience and expertise in helping me bring this project to completion. I am especially grateful to my editor, Fred Appel, who with extraordinary grace and wisdom has supported my writing and nurtured the thinking that has gone into producing this book. The anonymous readers who generously took the time to read my manuscript offered invaluable suggestions for improving it as a whole and rethinking key elements of individual chapters. I also thank my copyeditor, Martin Schneider, and Karen Carter, David Campbell, and James Collier at Princeton University Press for their superb work.

The writing of this book was supported in part by a life-changing Wallace Fellowship at Villa I Tatti, the Harvard University Center for Italian Renaissance Studies, in 2017. I extend my gratitude to the director, Alina Payne, and the marvelous staff at Villa I Tatti for all they did to make my time there so memorable. My fellowship in Florence would not have been possible without the help of Susan Elvin Cooper, Bard College Faculty Grants Officer. I thank her for her brilliant assistance in helping me craft my proposals and understand the larger principles involved in my research. Finally, I give my warmest thanks to my colleagues in Bard's Languages and Literature Division as well as the College's administration for all they have done to encourage and foster my work over the years.

This book is dedicated to my siblings in honor of our late parents, Pasquale and Yolanda Luzzi, who shared Dante's sense of what it means to leave one's homeland and build a new life elsewhere. Far from their native Calabria, they gave my brother and sisters and me the gift of the Italian culture they had left behind. And so, echoing Dante, I offer the words of this book *legato con amore in un volume*, bound together by love in a single volume, to my family.

Timeline

1265	Birth of Dante Alighieri
1302	Dante's exile from Florence
1304	Petrarch is born
1306	(c.) Dante begins the *Commedia*
1313	Birth of Boccaccio
1321	(c.) Completion of the *Commedia* Dante's death in Ravenna
1322	First commentary on *Inferno* is written, by Dante's son Jacopo
1327	Guido Vernani condemns Dante's *De monarchia*
1335	Vernani's Dominican Order bans the *Commedia*
1355	Boccaccio's first edition of his *Little Treatise in Praise of Dante* appears
1373–74	Boccaccio lectures on Dante in Florence
1374	Death of Petrarch
1375	Death of Boccaccio
1400	(c.) 827 manuscripts of *Commedia* are in circulation

1481	Landino's edition of the *Commedia* is printed in Florence
1481	(c.) Botticelli begins illustrations of the *Commedia*
1512	*Commedia* is published by Stagnino in Venice, later censured by the Inquisition
1564	*Commedia* is published by Sessa in Venice, later censured by the Inquisition
1576	*Editio princeps* of the *Vita nuova* is published
1629–1702	No editions of the *Commedia* are published
1667	Milton's *Paradise Lost* is published
1725	Vico discusses Dante in his letter to Gherardo degli Angioli
1755	Bettinelli writes *Virgilian Letters*, with attacks on Dante
1756	Voltaire proclaims, "Nobody reads Dante anymore"
1800–1850	181 editions of the *Commedia* are published in Europe
1803	Publication of Madame de Staël's *Corinne, or Italy*
1814	Cary's *The Vision*, a translation of the *Commedia*, appears
1818	Mary Shelley's *Frankenstein* is published anonymously
1820	Byron translates *Inferno* 5

1821	Shelley writes "A Defence of Poetry"
1823	Stendhal proclaims Dante the "Romantic poet par excellence"
1827	Manzoni goes to "rinse the laundry" in Dante's Arno
1865	Florence is named capital of Italy
	Cenotaph to Dante erected in Florence's Santa Croce on the six hundredth anniversary of poet's birth
1867	Longfellow completes the first American translation of *The Divine Comedy*
1871	Rome is named capital of Italy
1881	Dante Society of America is founded
1911	*L'Inferno* film is released in Italy
1912	Pound publishes a translation of Guido Cavalcanti's poetry
1914–21	Joyce writes *Ulysses*, which is published in the following year
1914	Eliot's "The Love Song of J. Alfred Prufrock" includes an epigraph from *Inferno* 27
1918	Gramsci references Dante in his article "The Blind Tiresias"
1921	Pope Benedict XV praises Dante in his encyclical letter "Among the Many Celebrated"
1933	Mandelstam writes "The Stalin Epigram"

1935	Spencer Tracy stars in *Dante's Inferno*
1947	Levi's *Se questo è un uomo* is published
1950–70	Some ten thousand articles are published on Dante
1991	Release of Kieślowski's film *The Double Life of Veronica*
2008	Florence city council votes to revoke Dante's exile by a 19–5 margin
2010	Release of *Dante's Inferno* video game
2012	Gherush92 attempts to ban the *Commedia*
2017	Zefferelli Foundation opens in Florence, with Dante Room
2021	Pope Francis publishes an apostolic letter on Dante
	Twitter hashtag #100daysofdante is created

Notes

In the interest of readability and concision, my general practice will be to cite Dante's *Commedia* and *Vita nuova* in the original and English translation, while other texts will be given in English translation only. When no other source is given, translations are my own.

Introduction

1. All references to Dante's text are to *La Commedia secondo l'antica vulgata*, ed. Giorgio Petrocchi, Edizione Nazionale della Società Dantesca Italiana, 4 vols. (Milan: Mondadori, 1966–67). All translations are from Dante, *The Divine Comedy*, trans. Allen Mandelbaum (New York: Everyman's Library, 1995). In a few cases, I have slightly modified Mandelbaum's translation; when I depart significantly from Mandelbaum's version, I will indicate the translation as my own in the notes.

2. The printer was Gabriele Giolito de' Ferrari, one of the first major publishers of literature in the Italian vernacular. For Dante's use of the term "comedìa," see *Inferno* 16.128, 21.2.

3. On the start date of composition, Lino Pertile remarks: "When did Dante begin his masterpiece? The consensus among modern scholars is that composition began in 1306–8. There is evidence that the three *cantiche* were released separately, one after the other, as they were completed: the *Inferno* after 1309, the *Purgatorio* after 1313, and the *Paradiso* in the last two or three years of the poet's life. Between the 'publication' of the *Inferno* and *Paradiso* there was a gap of eight to ten years." Pertile, "The *Commedia*," in *The Cambridge History of Italian Literature*, ed. Peter Brand and Lino Pertile (Cambridge: Cambridge University Press, 2008), 57

4. For a discussion of this key moment in the poem, see Dean Hadlow, *"La Nostra Effige": Dante and the Symbolism of the Human Form*, Ph.D. dissertation, La Trobe University, 2012, 17. For studies that underscore the image's synthesis of Aristotelian and Platonic elements, see Peter Dronke, "L'amor che move il sole e le altre stelle," *Studi medievali* 6 (1965): 389–90; and Zygmunt Barański, "L'esegesi medievali della

Commedia e il problema delle fonti," in *"Chiosar con altro testo": Leggere Dante nel Trecento* (Fiesole, Italy: Cadmo, 2001), 173–74, 217. For readings that point to the influence of the mystic Saint Bernard on Dante's rhetoric of loving oneself in God, see, among others, Robert Hollander, "The Invocations of the *Commedia*," *Yearbook of Italian Studies* 3 (1976): 35; and Christian Moevs, *The Metaphysics of Dante's "Comedy"* (Oxford: Oxford University Press, 2005), 81. For a study of Saint Bernard's presence in Dante's epic poem, see Steven Botterill, *Dante and the Mystical Tradition: Bernard of Clairvaux in the "Commedia"* (Cambridge: Cambridge University Press, 1994).

5. According to Christian tradition, Dante's vision of God was necessarily mediated because the only mortals granted full visual access to the Lord were, one, Moses, who engaged in sustained dialogue with God in the episode of the burning bush (Exodus 3:1–21) and also had a "face-to-face" encounter with Him (Moses 1:2); and two, Paul, who in the episode of his conversion described how he "had seen the Lord" and that "the Lord had spoken to him" (Acts 9:27). All biblical references are from the Holy Bible, New International Version (Biblica, 2011), www.biblegateway .com/.

6. See Dante, *Il Convivio (The Banquet)*, trans. Richard H. Lansing (New York: Garland Library of Medieval Literature, 1990).

7. Victor Hugo, *William Shakespeare*, trans. A. Baillot (Boston: Estes and Lauriat, 1864), book 2, chapter 2, section 11, Gutenberg.org, www.gutenberg.org/files/53490.

8. See Matthew Arnold, "The Study of Poetry" (1880), which describes "the simple, but perfect, single line—'In la sua volontade è nostra pace.'" Arnold appended a note: "In His will is our peace.—*Paradiso*, III, 85." Gutenberg.org, www .gutenberg.org/cache/epub/12628/pg12628-images.html.

9. See Robert Hollander, introduction to Dante Alighieri, *Paradiso*, trans. Robert and Jean Hollander (New York: Anchor Books, 2007), xx–xxi. For a more pop-cultural take on the challenges of *Paradiso*, see Robert Baird, "Paradise Lost: Why Doesn't Anyone Read Dante's *Paradiso*?," https://slate.com/culture/2007/12/why -doesn-t-anyone-read-dante-s-paradiso.html.

10. Joan M. Ferrante, "Dante's Beatrice: Priest of an Androgynous God," Bernardo Lecture Series, no. 2, Center for Medieval and Early Renaissance Studies, State University of New York, Binghamton, New York, 1992, 3.

11. Dante's excoriation of Pope Celestine V, a hermit who refused to perform his papal duties and abdicated five months after his election in July 1294, transpires within his critique of cowardly souls who never took sides in life:

> I saw and recognized the shade of him
> who made, through cowardice, the great refusal.
> *vidi e conobbi l'ombra di colui*
> *che fece per viltade il gran rifiuto.* (*Inf.* 3.59–60)

12. Bruno Nardi, "Whether Dante Was a True Prophet," trans. Marilyn Myatt, in *Critical Essays on Dante*, ed. Giuseppe Mazzotta (Englewood Cliffs, N.J.: Prentice Hall, 1991), 113. For Nardi's original text, see his *Dante e la cultura medievale: Nuovi saggi di filosofia dantesca* (Bari, Italy: Laterza, 1942), 318–26.

13. Nardi, "Whether Dante Was a True Prophet," 113.

14. Nardi, "Whether Dante Was a True Prophet," 114, 118–19.

15. Teodolinda Barolini, "Detheologizing Dante: For a 'New Formalism' in Dante Studies," *Quaderni d'italianistica* 10, nos. 1–2 (1989): 36. This article would form the basis of "Detheologizing Dante: Realism, Reception, and the Resources of Narrative," chapter 1 in *The Undivine Comedy: Detheologizing Dante* (Princeton: Princeton University Press, 1992), 3–20.

16. Charles S. Singleton, *Commedia: Elements of Structure* (Cambridge, Mass.: Harvard University Press, 1954), 62. According to Robert Hollander, Dante "creates a fiction which he pretends to consider not to be literally fictitious, while at the same time contriving to share the knowledge with us that it is precisely fictional." "Dante *Theologus-Poeta*," in *Studies in Dante* (Ravenna: Longo, 1980), 86.

17. Barolini, "Detheologizing Dante," 39.

18. Barolini, "Detheologizing Dante," 46.

19. Peter S. Hawkins, "Dante's 'Poema Sacro': No Either / Or," *Religion and Literature* 42, no. 3 (Autumn 2010): 145–46.

20. Peter S. Hawkins, "Dante's 'Poema Sacro,'" 146.

21. Peter S. Hawkins, "Dante's 'Poema Sacro,'" 146.

22. Harold Bloom, *Ruin the Sacred Truths: Poetry and Belief from the Bible to the Present* (Cambridge, Mass.: Harvard University Press, 1989), 45–46.

23. James Miller, "Retheologizing Dante," *Dante and the Unorthodox: The Aesthetics of Transgression*, ed. James Miller (Waterloo, Canada: Wilfrid Laurier University Press, 2005), 35–36.

24. William Franke, "Dante and the Secularization of Religion Through Literature," *Religion and Literature* 45, no. 1 (Spring 2013): 1.

25. Erich Auerbach, *Dante as Poet of the Secular World*, trans. Ralph Mannheim (New York: New York Review of Books, 2001). This relation between historical realism and transcendent religion was further developed by Auerbach in his seminal essay "Figura," in *Scenes from the Drama of European Literature* (Minneapolis: University of Minnesota Press, 1984), 11–76.

26. Francesco De Sanctis, "Francesca da Rimini," in *De Sanctis on Dante*, ed. and trans. Joseph Rossi and Alfred Galpin (Madison: University of Wisconsin Press, 1957), 36.

27. De Sanctis, "Francesca da Rimini," 51.

28. See Erich Auerbach, "Dante's Addresses to the Reader," *Romance Philology* 7 (1954): 268–78.

29. For a recent study of the philosophical issues surrounding Dante's addresses to the reader, especially in the light of hermeneutic theory, see William Franke, *Dante's Interpretive Journey* (Chicago: University of Chicago Press, 1996).

30. For a study and edition of this controversial work, see Robert Hollander's *Dante's Epistle to Cangrande* (Ann Arbor: University of Michigan, 1993), which argues that the letter is authentically Dante's; on where scholars stand on the issue, see 100; and for mention of those with opposing views, 44.

31. For a summary of interpretations of the *selva oscura*, see Anthony K. Cassell, *Lectura Dantis Americana: Inferno I* (Philadelphia: University of Pennsylvania Press, 1989), 14–18. See also Robert Pogue Harrison, *Forests: The Shadow of Civilization* (Chicago: University of Chicago Press, 1992), 82; and Lawrence Warner, "The Dark Wood and the Dark Word in Dante's 'Commedia,'" *Comparative Literature Studies* 32, no. 4 (1995): 449–78.

32. See Enzo Esposito, *Bibliografia analitica degli scritti su Dante dal 1950 al 1970* (Florence: Olschki, 1990), 5; and Christopher Kleinhenz and Kristina Olson, eds., *Approaches to Teaching Dante's "Divine Comedy"* (New York: Modern Language Association of America, 2020).

33. T. S. Eliot, *Dante* (London: Faber and Faber, 1929), 51.

34. The recent variety and richness of Dante studies have transformed the study of the poet in a range of topics and forms outside of the traditional Western literary canon. For an anthology that showcases Dante's broad impact in many different cultural domains, see Francesco Ciabattoni and Simone Marchesi, eds., *Dante Alive: Essays on a Cultural Icon* (London: Routledge, 2022). For another edited volume that presents new trends and approaches in Dante criticism, see Manuele Gragnolati, Elena Lombardi, and Francesca Southerden, eds., *The Oxford Handbook of Dante* (Oxford: Oxford University Press, 2021). The history of Dante in translation has been charted by Peter Hainsworth and David Robey in "Translating Dante 1966–2019," in *Dante Beyond Borders: Contexts and Reception*, ed. Nick Havely and Jonathan Katz with Richard Cooper (Cambridge: Legenda, 2021), 349–62. For Dante's presence among Middle Eastern cultures, see Valerio Cappozzo, "Dante and Islam, Islam and Dante," in the same volume, 157–68. For a study of Dante's historical influence among Black Americans, see Dennis Looney, *Freedom Readers: The African American Reception of Dante Alighieri and the* Divine Comedy (Notre Dame: University of Notre Dame Press, 2017). Readings that feature Dante's presence in American political thought include Deborah Parker, "The Historical Presidency: JFK's Dante," *Presidential Studies Quarterly* 48 (June 2018): 357–72; Akash Kumar, "Teddy Roosevelt, Dante, and the Man in the Arena," *Digital Dante*, Columbia University Libraries, 2018, https://digitaldante.columbia.edu/history/teddy-roosevelt-dante-kumar/; and Kristina Olson, "'Maintaining Neutrality in a Period of Moral Crisis': The Appropriation of

Inferno 3 from JFK to Martha Nussbaum," in *Dante Beyond Borders*, ed. Havely et al., 311–23. Scholarship on Dante's pop-cultural manifestations may be found in Nancy J. Vickers, "Dante in the Video Decade," in *Dante Now: Current Trends in Dante Studies*, ed. Theodore J. Cachey (Notre Dame: Notre Dame University Press, 1995), 263–76; and Deborah Parker and Mark Parker, *Inferno Revealed: From Dante to Dan Brown* (New York: Palgrave Macmillan, 2013). An online resource that attests to Dante's pop-cultural appeal is Arielle Saiber and Elizabeth Coggeshall, eds., *Dante Today: Citings and Sightings of Dante's Works in Contemporary Culture*, https://dantetoday.krieger.jhu .edu/. For Dante's presence in nonliterary art forms, see Antonella Braida and Luisa Calè, eds., *Dante on View: The Reception of Dante in the Visual and Performing Arts* (London: Ashgate, 2007); and Otfried Lieberknecht, "Dante's Reception in Music," *The Princeton Dante Project*, https://dante.princeton.edu/pdp/da_mu.htm.

35. See Jorge Luis Borges, "The Divine Comedy," in *The Poets' Dante*, ed. Peter S. Hawkins and Rachel Jacoff (New York: Farrar, Straus and Giroux, 2001), 126.

36. See "topos," *Merriam-Webster.com Dictionary*, Merriam-Webster, www .merriam-webster.com/dictionary/topos.

37. The work appeared in translation as Ernst Robert Curtius, *European Literature and the Latin Middle Ages*, trans. Willard Trask (Princeton: Princeton University Press, 1953).

38. See the discussion of Curtius in Paolo A. Cherchi, "Tradition and Topoi in Medieval Literature," *Critical Inquiry* 3, no. 2 (Winter 1976): 285.

39. For the articulation of these views, see Moretti's two seminal articles: "Conjectures on World Literature," *New Left Review* 1 (2000): 54–68; and "The Slaughterhouse of Literature," *Modern Language Quarterly* 61, no. 1 (2000): 207–27.

40. For studies of Birk's illustrations, see Kristina Olson, "Dante in a Global World: Sandow Birk's *Divine Comedy*," in *Unexpected Dante*, ed. Lucia Wolf (Lewisburg, Penn.: Bucknell University Press, 2021), 47–59; and Akash Kumar, "Vernacular Hybridity Across Borders: Dante, Amīr Khusrau, Sandow Birk," in *Dante Beyond Borders*, ed. Havely et al., 338–48.

41. For discussion of Dante's "encyclopedic" vision, see Giuseppe Mazzotta, *Dante's Vision and the Circle of Knowledge* (Princeton: Princeton University Press, 1993).

42. The original reads: "piangendo disse: 'Se per questo cieco / carcere vai per altezza d' ingegno, / mio figlio ov' è? e perché non è teco?'"

43. For a summary of the vast critical literature on the topic of *cui* and its referent, see my "Echoes of Andromache in *Inferno* X," *Dante Studies* 122 (2004): 39n1.

44. References to the text are from P. B. Shelley, "A Defence of Poetry and Other Essays," Gutenberg.org, www.gutenberg.org/files/5428/5428-h/5428-h.htm.

45. Dante, *De Vulgari Eloquentia*, ed. and trans. Steven Botterill (Cambridge: Cambridge University Press, 1993), 2.4.2. For a discussion of Dante's relation to

188 NOTES TO CHAPTER 1

music, see Patrick Boyde, "Dante Alighieri," Grove Music Online, www.oxford
musiconline.com; and Francesco Ciabbatoni, *Dante's Journey to Polyphony* (Toronto:
University of Toronto Press, 2014).

46. For discussion of the Augustinian element in Dante, see especially Freccero's classic essay "The Prologue Scene," in *Dante: The Poetics of Conversion*, ed.
Rachel Jacoff (Cambridge, Mass.: Harvard University Press, 1986), 1–28. Freccero
revisits issues in this essay, including concerns with allegory and the tension between poetry and theology in Dante's autobiographical narrative, in "Allegory and
Autobiography," in *The Cambridge Companion to Dante*, ed. Rachel Jacoff (Cambridge: Cambridge University Press, 2007), 161–80. On the opening page Freccero
writes: "The conversion from presumption to humility is also the theme of Dante's
descent into Hell, which likewise takes place in middle age: 'nel mezzo del cammin
di nostra vita.' The landscape of the prologue scene borrows several details from
book 7 of Augustine's *Confessions*, where philosophical presumption is distinguished from confession: 'it is one thing, from a wooded mountain top, to see the
land of peace and quite another to reach it, when one's way is beset by the lion and
the dragon.'"

47. Dante, *Vita nuova*, ed. Michele Barbi (Florence: Bemporad, 1932), 1.1. Translations are from Mark Musa, ed., *Dante's "Vita Nuova"* (Bloomington: Indiana University Press, 1973). In some instances, I have modified Musa's translations slightly.

48. Curtius describes the *Vita nuova*, an unusual combination of lyric poetry and
narrative that anthologizes the range of Dante's poetic compositions from his late
teenage to early adult years, as one of the first "books" in the Middle Ages. *European
Literature and the Latin Middle Ages*, 326–28.

49. Dante, *Vita nuova*, 1.1.

Chapter 1: Inventing "Italian" Literature

1. Dante, *Vita nuova* 25: "prima è da intendere che anticamente non erano dicitori
d'amore in lingua volgare, anzi erano dicitori d'amore certi poete in lingua latina; tra
noi dico, avvegna forse che tra altra gente addivenisse, e addivegna ancora, sì come
in Grecia, non volgari ma litterati poete queste cose trattavano."

2. For a discussion of Dante's contributions to the creation of a vernacular literary
tradition in fourteenth-century Italy, see Martin Eisner, *Boccaccio and the Invention
of Italian Literature: Dante, Petrarch, Cavalcanti, and the Authority of the Vernacular*
(Cambridge: Cambridge University Press, 2013), 29–31.

3. The term comes from the German poet Novalis. See the discussion in Geoffrey H. Hartman, *Scars of the Spirit: The Struggle Against Inauthenticity* (London:
Palgrave Macmillan, 2002), 164–65.

4. Jacob Burckhardt, *The Civilization of the Renaissance in Italy*, trans. S. G. C. Middlemoore (London: Penguin, 1990), 137; Dante, *Vita nuova* 25.

5. Dante, *Vita nuova* 25: "dico che né li poete parlavano così sanza ragione, né quelli che rìmano dèono parlare così, non avendo alcuno ragionamento in loro di quello che dicono." See also his words in this same chapter on "some who compose so clumsily"; "quelli che rimano stoltamente."

6. I discuss this tension between Dante's personal journey ("I found myself," *mi ritrovai, Inf.* 1.2) and our common human experience ("our life," *nostra vita, Inf.* 1.1) in the opening lines of *Inferno* in my *In a Dark Wood: What Dante Taught Me About Grief, Healing, and the Mysteries of Love* (New York: HarperCollins, 2015), 1. For more on Dante's concluding imagery in the *Paradiso* and its sources, see note 4 in the introduction above.

7. See Christopher Duggan, *La Forza del Destino: A History of Italy Since 1796* (Boston: Houghton Mifflin, 2008), 241.

8. I explore this point in *My Two Italies* (New York: Farrar, Straus and Giroux, 2014), 109. See also Dante's words on how the illustrious vernacular, one, digs up daily "thorn bushes growing in the Italian forest"; and two, exemplifies how "the best language is suited to the best thinking." *De Vulgari Eloquentia*, 43, 49.

9. I discuss this passage from Adam, and its relation to the subtext from Horace, in "'As a Leaf on a Branch . . .': Dante's Neologisms," *PMLA* 125, no. 2 (2010): 329.

10. Auerbach, *Literary Language*, 47.

11. Auerbach, *Literary Language*, 312.

12. Auerbach, *Literary Language*, 317.

13. For a discussion of the 827 circulating manuscripts of Dante's work in the 1300s, see Marcella Roddewig, *Dante Alighieri: Die "Göttliche Komödie": Vergleichende Bestandsaufnahme der "Commedia"-Handschriften* (Stuttgart: Anton Hiersemann, 1984). See also Gabriella Pomaro, "*Commedia*: Editions," trans. Robin Treasure, in *The Dante Encyclopedia*, ed. Lansing, 201–6; and John Ahern, "What Did the First Copies of the *Comedy* Look Like?," in *Dante for the New Millennium*, ed. Teodolinda Barolini and H. Wayne Storey (New York: Fordham University Press, 2003), 1–15.

14. Paola Nasti and Claudia Rossignoli, *Interpreting Dante: Essays on the Traditions of Dante Commentary*, ed. Nasti and Rossignoli (Notre Dame: Notre Dame University Press, 2013), i.

15. Nasti and Rossignoli, *Interpreting Dante*, i.

16. Fourteenth-century commentaries included Jacopo Alighieri (1322), Graziolo Bambaglioli (1324), Iacomo della Lana (1324–28), Guido da Pisa (c. 1333–40), Ottimo (1334), Pietro Alighieri (three versions, 1340–64), Chiose Ambrosiane (c. 1355), Guglielmo Maramauro (1369–73), Giovanni Boccaccio (1373–74), Benvenuto da Imola (1379–83), Francesco da Buti (1396), and Filippo Villani (1391–1405). See Saverio

Bellomo, "How to Read Early Commentaries," in *Interpreting Dante,* ed. Nasti and Rossignoli, 85–86. For a full list of commentaries on Dante, see the Dartmouth Dante Project, https://dante.dartmouth.edu/commentaries.php.

17. On the methodology of Dante's earliest commentators, Steven Botterill writes: "Though they vary in their choice of language, their analytical approach, and the closeness of their treatment of different parts of the poem, what they produce are, essentially, annotations: self-contained bits of commentary that appear sporadically in relation to Dante's continuous text, as inspired by the perceived need for interpretation or explication, and which clearly reveal, in their brevity, their specificity, and, in some manuscripts, still in their arrangement on the page, their origin as literally interlinear or marginal observations." "Reading, Writing, and Speech in the Fourteenth-and Fifteenth-Century Commentaries on Dante's *Comedy,*" in *Interpreting Dante,* ed. Nasti and Rossignoli, 19.

18. Latin translations of the Homeric epic would not appear in Europe until the fifteenth century. Before then, most medieval readers had access to Homer primarily through the *Ilias latina* (Latin *Iliad*), a crude condensation of the *Iliad* into 1,070 lines of Latin hexameter. The work is attributed to Publius Baebius Italicus, c. 60–70 AD. See Curtius, *European Literature and the Latin Middle Ages,* 49.

19. On the extraordinary number of parallels between the two works, see Alyssa Granacki, "Dante's Teacher: Brunetto Latini, *Trésor,*" https://sites.duke.edu /danteslibrary/brunetto-latini-tresor/.

20. For a study of Boccaccio's influence on the development of Renaissance scholarship on Dante, see Jason Houston, *Building a Monument to Dante: Boccaccio as Dantista* (Toronto: University of Toronto Press, 2011).

21. Giovanni Boccaccio, "Life of Dante," in *The Early Lives of Dante,* trans. Philip Wicksteed (New York: Henry Holt, 1904), 10.

22. Boccaccio, "Life of Dante," 11.

23. For Petrarch's epistolary response to Boccaccio and its accompanying critique of Dante, see *Familiarium rerum libri,* in *Prose,* ed. Enrico Bianchi (Milan: Riccardo Ricciardi, 1955), 21.15, 1002–14.

24. After Dante introduces himself to the poet Bonagiunta da Lucca as "one who, when Love breathes in him, takes note" in *Purgatorio* 24, Bonagiunta replies memorably, naming Petrarch's oft-maligned Guittone d'Arezzo along the way:

"O brother, now I see," he said, "the knot
that kept the Notary, Guittone, and me
short of the sweet new manner that I hear."
"O frate, issa vegg' io", diss' elli, "il nodo
che 'l Notaro e Guittone e me ritenne
di qua dal dolce stil novo ch'i' odo!" (55–57)

25. Giovanni Boccaccio, *Genealogy of the Pagan Gods*, ed. and trans. Jon Solomon, 2 vols. (Cambridge, Mass.: I Tatti Renaissance Library, 2017), 14.4.12.

26. Boccaccio, *Genealogy of the Pagan Gods*, 14.4.12; and Petrarch, *Familiarium rerum libri*, 21.15, 1008. See also Michael Papio, *Boccaccio's Expositions on Dante's* Comedy (Toronto: Toronto University Press, 2009), 9.

27. See Martin McLaughlin, "Humanism and Italian Literature," in *The Cambridge Companion to Renaissance Humanism*, ed. Jill Kraye (Cambridge: Cambridge University Press, 1996), 226.

28. I will limit myself to a selection of key works on the subject: Robert Hollander, *Boccaccio's Dante and the Shaping Force of Satire* (Ann Arbor: University of Michigan Press, 1997); Kristina Olson, *Courtesy Lost: Dante, Boccaccio, and the Literature of History* (Toronto: University of Toronto Press, 2014); Gur Zak, "Boccaccio and Petrarch," in *The Cambridge Companion to Boccaccio*, ed. Guyda Armstrong et al. (Cambridge: Cambridge University Press, 2015), 139–54; Eisner, *Boccaccio and the Invention of Italian Literature.* On Petrarch's and Boccaccio's attitude toward Dante's legacy, see Oskar Hecker, *Boccaccio-Funde* (Brauschweig, Germany: G. Westermann. 1902), 3–4, 12, 26; and Giuseppe Billanovich, "Tra Dante e Petrarca," in *Italia Medievale e Umanistica* 8 (1965): 1–44; Billanovich, *Lo scrittoio del Petrarca*, vol. 1 of *Petrarca letterato* (Rome: Edizioni di Storia e Letteratura, 1995), 147–48. For a résumé of works on Petrarch's attitude toward Dante, see Nancy J. Vickers, "Dante: Petrarch's 'Chiare, fresche et dolci acque,'" *MLN: Italian Issue* 96, no. 1 (January 1981): 2n2. More recently, see Zygmunt G. Barański and Theodore Cachey Jr., eds., *Petrarch and Dante: Anti-Dantism, Metaphysics, Tradition* (Notre Dame: University of Notre Dame Press, 2009). On the differences between Petrarch's and Boccaccio's views on the vernacular, Simona Lorenzini writes: "The world of Boccaccio is a world open to many influences, Latin and vernacular alike; it is rich and varied in its instability and defies all rigid and absolute interpretative schemes. By contrast, Petrarch's elitism and exclusivity are reflected in his choice of Latin and in his personal debate with Dante. Each model is equally valid, even though Petrarch's beautiful poetic translation forfeits the complexity of Boccaccio's ironic gaze on human comedy. The debate regarding Dante and vernacular literature leads to a positive outcome for Boccaccio; for Petrarch, instead, it remains unresolved." Lorenzini, "Petrarch and Boccaccio: The Rewriting of Griselda's Tale (*Dec.* 10.10). A Rhetorical Debate on Latin and Vernacular Languages," *Heliotropia* 16–17 (2019–20): 222–23.

29. On the professional class of merchants and notaries who copied, preserved, and circulated Dante's poetry, see Justin Steinberg, *Accounting for Dante: Urban Readers and Writers in Late Medieval Italy* (Notre Dame: University of Notre Dame Press, 2007).

Chapter 2: *Comedìa Proibita*

1. On the "chiastic" structure of *Paradiso* 11–12, see Barolini, *The Undivine Comedy*, 200.

2. Vernani's tract was not published until 1741; for more recent critical editions, see T. Käppeli, ed., "Der Dantegegner Guido Vernani, O.P. von Rimini," *Quellen und Forschungen aus italienischen Archiven und Bibliotheken* 28 (1938): 107–46; and Nevio Matteini, ed., *Il più antico oppositore politico di Dante: Guido Vernani da Rimini. Testo critico del "De reprobatione monarchiae"* (Padua, Italy: CEDAM, 1958).

3. See Teodolinda Barolini, Commento Baroliniano [Commentary by Barolini], *Digital Dante*, Columbia University Libraries, 2018, https://digitaldante.columbia.edu/dante/divine-comedy/purgatorio/purgatorio-16/. Refuting the "sun-moon" paradigm of political thinking, Dante writes: "Thus I say that the temporal realm does not owe its existence to the spiritual realm, nor its power (which is its authority), and not even its function in an absolute sense; but it does receive from it the capacity to operate more efficaciously through the light of grace which in heaven and on earth the blessing of the supreme Pontiff infuses into it." *Monarchia* 3.4.20.

References are to Dante's *Monarchia*, ed. Pier Giorgio Ricci, vol. 5 of *Le opere di Dante Alighieri* (Milan: Mondadori, 1965). English translations are from *Monarchy*, ed. and trans. Prue Shaw (Cambridge: Cambridge University Press, 1996).

4. Vernani, *Refutation of the Monarchia Composed by Dante*, 174. All references to the text are to the chapter "Here Begins the Treatise of Friar Guido Vernani of the Order of Preachers, Concerning *The Refutation of the Monarchia* Composed by Dante," in Anthony K. Cassell, *The Monarchia Controversy: An Historical Study with Accompanying Translations of Dante Alighieri's "Monarchia," Guido Vernani's "Refutation of the Monarchia Composed by Dante," and Pope John XXII's bull, "Si fratrum"* (Washington, D.C.: Catholic University of America Press, 2004), 174–97.

5. Vernani, *Refutation*, 175.

6. Vernani, *Refutation*, 174.

7. Vernani *Refutation*, 179.

8. Vernani, *Refutation*, 180.

9. Vernani, *Refutation*, 180.

10. For discussion of how "Dante was attached, simultaneously, to Christianity and to paganism," see Kenelm Foster, *The Two Dantes* (London: Darton, Longman and Todd, 1977), 156. On Dante's political thinking and its relation to ancient Roman history, see Charles Till Davis, *Dante and the Idea of Rome* (Oxford: Clarendon Press, 1959), esp. chapter 1, "Dante and the Roman Past," 40–138; and Joan M. Ferrante, *The Political Vision of the "Divine Comedy"* (Princeton: Princeton University Press, 1984), esp. chapter 1, "City and Empire in the *Comedy*," 44–75.

11. Vernani, *Refutation*, 182.

12. Augustine, *Confessions*, trans. Henry Chadwick (Oxford: Oxford University Press, 2009). Compare Augustine's critique of Virgil to Dante's paean to this guide:

> "And are you then that Virgil, you the fountain
> that freely pours so rich a stream of speech?"
> I answered him with shame upon my brow.
> "O light and honor of all other poets,
> may my long study and the intense love
> that made me search your volume serve me now.
> You are my master and my author, you—
> the only one from whom my writing drew
> the noble style for which I have been honored."
>
> *"Or se' tu quel Virgilio e quella fonte*
> *che spandi di parlar sì largo fiume?",*
> *rispuos' io lui con vergognosa fronte.*
> *"O de li altri poeti onore e lume*
> *vagliami 'l lungo studio e 'l grande amore*
> *che m'ha fatto cercar lo tuo volume.*
> *Tu se' lo mio maestro e 'l mio autore;*
> *tu se' solo colui da cu' io tolsi*
> *lo bello stilo che m'ha fatto onore."* (*Inf.* 1.79–87)

13. Vernani, *Refutation*, 188.

14. Vernani, *Refutation*, 192.

15. See Acts 8:9–24; and Dante, *Inf.* 19.1–3:

> "O Simon Magus! O his sad disciples!
> Rapacious ones, who take the things of God,
> that ought to be the brides of Righteousness."
>
> *"O Simon mago, o miseri seguaci*
> *che le cose di Dio, che di bontate*
> *deon essere spose, e voi rapaci."*

16. See Foster, *Two Dantes*, 89. More broadly, see Gary P. Cestaro, "Boniface VIII, Pope," in *Medieval Italy: An Encyclopedia*, ed. Christopher Kleinhenz (New York: Routledge, 2004), 143–44.

17. Barolini adds: "By damning Boniface before he died in 1303, Dante effectively denies him the possibility of repentance *in extremis*. . . . Most important, he denies Boniface's free will, the agency gifted by God that allows sinners to repent and convert to the good throughout life, as long as one is alive." Commento Baroliniano, "Whoring the Bride," *Digital Dante*, https://digitaldante.columbia.edu/dante/divine-comedy/inferno/inferno-19/.

18. Vernani, *Refutation*, 194.

19. Vernani, *Refutation*, 195.

20. Vernani, *Refutation*, 197.

21. Cassell, *Monarchia Controversy*.

22. See Joan M. Ferrante, "Hell as the Mirror Image of *Paradise*," in *Dante's Inferno, The Indiana Critical Edition*, ed. Mark Musa (Bloomington: Indiana University Press, 1995), 368.

23. Hawkins, "Dante's 'Poema Sacro,'" 146.

24. For the basic details of Beatrice Portinari's life and her role in Dante's work, see Aldo Vallone, "Beatrice," in *Enciclopedia dantesca*, ed. Umberto Bosco, 6 vols. (Rome: Istituto dell'Enciclopedia Italiana, 1970–76), 1:542–51. For a study of how Boccaccio has influenced our notions of Beatrice, see James H. McGregor, "Is Beatrice Boccaccio's Most Successful Fiction?," *Texas Studies in Literature and Language* 32, no. 1, special issue: *Beatrice Dolce Memoria, 1290–1990: Essays on the Vita Nuova and the Beatrice-Dante Relationship* (Spring 1990): 137–51. In the same issue, Joy Hambuechen, who reads the *Vita nuova* in terms of a "power struggle" between Dante and Beatrice in which the poet-protagonist attempts to free himself from the destructive love he feels for his tragic muse. Hambuechen, "Beatrice, Dead or Alive: Love in the 'Vita Nuova,'" 32, no. 1 (Spring 1990): 60–84.

25. For discussion of this volume, see Aaron Wirth, "Dante's *Divine Comedy* Censored by the Spanish Inquisition," www.brandeis.edu/library/archives/essays /special-collections/dante.html.

26. Translation in Wirth, "Dante's *Divine Comedy* Censored by the Spanish Inquisition."

27. See Elspeth Healey, "Banned Books Week: Redacted for the Inquisition," *Inside Spencer: The KSRL Blog*, September 28, 2017, https://blogs.lib.ku.edu /spencer/banned-books-week-redacted-for-the-inquisition/. Transcriptions and translations are by Luis Corteguera, with assistance from Patricia Manning and Isidro Rivera.

28. See Witte's edition of the *Vita nuova* (Leipzig: F. A. Brockhaus, 1876), 22.4.

29. See the discussion in Paget Toynbee, "The Inquisition and the 'Editio Princeps' of the 'Vita Nuova,'" *Modern Language Review* 3, no. 3 (April 1908): 229. This edition also contained Boccaccio's *Little Treatise in Praise of Dante*—which, as no less a reader than John Milton observed in his commonplace book, was also censored by the Inquisition. See Toynbee, "Earliest References to Dante in English Literature," in *Miscellanea di studi critici edita in onore di Arturo Graf* (Bergamo, Italy: Istituto Italiano di Arte Grafiche, 1903).

30. Toynbee, "The Inquisition and the 'Editio Princeps' of the 'Vita Nuova,'" 230.

31. Toynbee calls this the "most cruel and senseless mutilation" of the *Vita nuova*. "The Inquisition and the 'Editio Princeps' of the 'Vita Nuova,'" 230–31.

32. Teodolinda Barolini, "Why Did Dante Write the *Commedia*? or the Vision Thing," *Dante Studies* 111 (1993): 3.

33. Barolini, "Why Did Dante Write the *Commedia*?," 3. Barolini urges us to read Dante in that same visionary tradition from which he is often excluded because, she argues, his poetry surpasses the more rhetorically crude and simple visionary precursors to his *Commedia* in the Middle Ages by his contemporaries (4).

Chapter 3: Renaissance Visions

1. Among the vast amount of scholarship on this issue, see Leonard Foster, *The Icy Fire: Five Studies in European Petrarchism* (Cambridge: Cambridge University Press, 1969); William J. Kennedy, *The Site of Petrarchism: Early Modern National Sentiment in Italy, France, and England* (Baltimore: Johns Hopkins University Press, 2004); and Roland Greene, *Post-Petrarchism: Origins and Innovations of the Western Lyric Sequence* (Princeton: Princeton University Press, 2016). For an understanding of the tensions between Petrarch's humanist philosophy and more personal issues of identity, see Gur Zak, *Petrarch's Humanism and the Care of the Self* (Cambridge: Cambridge University Press, 2010); and for a historical perspective on the broader issue of Renaissance humanism that Petrarch helped initiate, see Charles G. Nauert, *Humanism and the Culture of Renaissance Europe* (Cambridge: Cambridge University Press, 2006).

2. On this subject, see Simon Gilson, *Dante and Renaissance Florence* (Cambridge: Cambridge University Press, 2005); and, more broadly, Gilson, *Reading Dante in Renaissance Italy: Florence, Venice, and the "Divine Poet"* (Cambridge: Cambridge University Press, 2018).

3. For Bruni's words, see David Thompson and Alan F. Nagel, eds., *The Three Crowns of Florence: Humanist Assessments of Dante, Petrarca, and Boccaccio* (New York: Harper and Row, 1972), 82.

4. See Peter H. Brieger, Millard Meiss, and Charles S. Singleton, *Illuminated Manuscripts of the* Divine Comedy (Princeton: Princeton University Press, 1969).

5. For a study of Michelangelo's vast knowledge of Dante (whom he reputedly "knew almost by heart"), see Peter Armour, "'A ciascun artista l'ultimo suo': Dante and Michelangelo," *Lectura Dantis*, 22–23, special issue: *Visibile Parlare: Dante and the Art of the Italian Renaissance* (Spring and Fall 1998): 141–80, esp. 141. The legend of the supposed Dante competition between Leonardo and Michelangelo comes from the sixteenth-century author known as the Anonymous Magliabechiano.

6. The writing for this chapter expands on research and ideas that I originally developed in *Botticelli's Secret: The Lost Drawings and the Rediscovery of the Renaissance* (New York: W. W. Norton, 2022).

7. The identity of the graphic artist who made these rather clumsy adaptations of Botticelli's beautiful drawings remains a mystery. Most believe him to be Bacio Baldini.

8. In a testament to Dante's ongoing inspiration for visual artists, Cristoforo Landino was featured in the Japanese *manga* artist Fuyumo Soryo's "Cesare: Il creatore che ha distrutto," which dedicates a chapter to Landino's lecture to Cesare Borgia and Giovanni de' Medici (the future Leo X) at the University of Pisa. See Deborah Parker, "The Dante Lesson in Fuyumi Soryo's 'Cesare: Il creatore che ha distrutto,'" *Bibliotheca Dantesca: Journal of Dante Studies* 4, article 2; https://repository.upenn.edu/bibdant/vol4/iss1/2.

9. Brunelleschi used a series of mirrors to create a perfectly measured painting of Florence's Baptistery. There was a hole in the painting's canvas that enabled the viewer to match the physical location of the building with its visual representation, thus establishing a direct one-point perspective between the painter and his painted object. For a description of the groundbreaking experiment, see Ross King, *Brunelleschi's Dome: How a Renaissance Genius Reinvented Architecture* (New York: Bloomsbury, 2013), 35–36.

10. For Vasari's full account of Botticelli, see his *Lives of the Artists: Volume I*, trans. George Bull (London: Penguin, 1987), 224–31.

11. The translation is mine.

12. See Hein-Th. Schulze Altcappenberg, ed., *Sandro Botticelli: The Drawings for Dante's "Divine Comedy,"* 136.

13. See Erich Auerbach's moving words, echoing Hegel, on the "changeless existence" of the souls in Dante's afterlife. "Farinata and Cavalcante," in *Mimesis: The Representation of Reality in Literature*, trans. Willard Trask (Princeton: Princeton University Press, 1953), 191.

14. "Trattando l'ombra come cosa salda" (*Purg.* 24.130). See the work on embraces and identity by Manuele Gragnolati, "Nostalgia in Heaven: Embraces, Affection, and Identity in Dante's *Commedia*," in *Dante and the Human Body*, ed. John Barnes and Jennifer Petrie (Dublin: Four Courts Press, 2007), 91–111.

15. See Baxandall's classic study *Painting and Experience in Fifteenth-Century Italy: A Primer in the Social History of Pictorial Style* (Oxford: Oxford University Press, 1988).

16. See Alessandro Cecchi, *Botticelli* (Florence: Federico Motta, 2005), 62; as well as Poliziano's descriptions of Botticelli's sharp wit in *Detti piacevoli*, ed. Tiziano Zanati (Rome: Istituto dell'Enciclopedia Italiana, 1983), nos. 328, 366.

17. Bernard Berenson, "Botticelli's Illustrations to the *Divina Commedia*," *The Nation*, November 12, 1896, 363–64, reprinted in Henry M. Christman, ed., *One Hundred Years of the Nation: A Centennial Anthology* (New York: Macmillan, 1965), 91–95.

18. Herbert Horne, *Botticelli, Painter of Florence* (Princeton: Princeton University Press, 1980), 238.

19. For Whitehead's quote, see Richard John Neuhaus, *Death on a Friday Afternoon* (New York: Basic Books, 2000), 5.

20. Dante's extensive use of neologisms in *Paradiso* is the subject of my "'As a Leaf.'"

21. The translation is mine.

22. I review this theory—and offer my support for it—in *Botticelli's Secret*, 107.

23. Berenson, "Botticelli's Illustrations to the *Divina Commedia*," 364.

24. "condescende / a vostra facultate" (*Par.* 4.43–44).

25. On Dante's understanding of gestures and bodily signs, see Heather Webb, *Dante, Artist of Gesture* (Oxford: Oxford University Press, 2022).

26. Thomas Thomas used the phrase "personages of great estate" in his dictionary definition of *tragedy* from the 1580s; cited in Sylvan Barnet, introduction to William Shakespeare, *Four Great Tragedies: Hamlet, Othello, King Lear, Macbeth*, ed. Barnet (New York: Signet, 1998), v.

27. See Androniki Dialeti, "The Publisher Gabriel Giolito de' Ferrari, Female Readers, and the Debate About Women in Sixteenth-Century Italy," *Renaissance and Reformation / Renaissance et Réforme* 28, no. 4 (Fall 2004): 7.

28. See Louise George Clubb and William G. Clubb, "Building a Lyric Canon: Gabriel Giolito and the Rival Anthologists, 1545–1590: Part I," *Italica* 68, no. 3 (Autumn 1991): 332.

Chapter 4: The Lost Centuries

1. See *Dante*, ed. Caesar, 35.

2. See *Dante*, ed. Caesar, 35.

3. See *Dante*, ed. Caesar, 36–37.

4. See *Dante*, ed. Caesar, 38.

5. A multitude of commentaries were produced during the Renaissance, including Filippo Villani (1405), Johannis de Serravalle (1416–17), Guiniforto delli Barini (1440), Cristoforo Landino (1481), Alessandro Vellutello (1544), Pier Francesco Giumballari (1538–48), Benedetto Varchi (1545), Trifon Gabriele (1525–41), Bernardino Daniello (1547–68), and the great epic poet Torquato Tasso (1555–68). For analysis of the Renaissance commentary tradition on Dante, see Deborah Parker, *Commentary and Ideology in the Renaissance* (Durham, N.C.: Duke University Press, 1993).

6. Tommaso Campanella, *Scritti letterari*, vol. 1 of *Tutte le opere*, ed. Luigi Firpo (Milan: Mondadori, 1954), 341.

7. Campanella, *Poëtica*, in *Scritti lettari*, 1169.

8. Voltaire, *Correspondence and Related Documents*, ed. Theodore Besterman, in *The Complete Works of Voltaire*, vols. 85–135 (Geneva: Voltaire Foundation, 1968–77), D8663. For Voltaire's Shakespearean insult, see vol. 4 in *Oeuvres complètes de Voltaire*, ed. Louis Moland, 52 vols. (Paris: Garnier, 1882), 501–3.

9. See, for example, Dante's infamous joke in *Inf.* 21.139: "ed elli avea del cul fatto trombetta"; "And [the demon] had made a trumpet of his ass."

10. For a thorough study of the relation between Milton's writing and Dante's, see Irene Samuel, *Dante and Milton: The* Commedia *and* Paradise Lost (Ithaca, N.Y.: Cornell University Press, 1966). See also Oscar Kuhns, "Dante's Influence on Milton," *Modern Language Notes* 13, no. 1 (January 1898): 2.

11. On Milton's relationship with Diodati and his early exposure to the Italian language, see A. N. Wilson, *The Life of John Milton* (Oxford: Oxford University Press, 1983), 14–16; on Milton's Italian poetry, see Francisco Nahoe, "The Italian Verse of Milton," Ph.D. dissertation, University of Nevada, Reno, 2018.

12. See Wilson, *Life of John Milton*, 90. On Milton's Florentine sojourn and the intellectual contacts the English poet made there, especially with the prolific Dante commentator Benedetto Buonmattei, see A. M. Cinquemani, *Glad to Go for a Feast: Milton, Buonmattei, and the Florentine Accademici* (New York: Peter Lang, 1998), esp. 117–58.

13. The full title of this *editio princeps* is: *Vita nuova di Dante Alighieri. Con XV canzoni del medesimo. E la vita di esso Dante scritta da Giovanni Boccaccio* (Florence: Bartolomeo Sermartelli, 1576).

14. For the full tabulations, see Mark Akenside, "Ballance of the Poets," *The Museum*, vol. 19, December 6, 1746, 165–69.

15. For a list of the more than fifty "parallel passages" in Milton's *Paradise Lost* and Dante's *Commedia*, see Paget Toynbee, *Dante in English Literature from Chaucer to Gray (c. 1380–1844)* (London: Methuen, 1909), 127–28.

16. See Samuel's point that "Dante and Milton both recognize a problem in man's exercise of choice." *Dante and Milton*, 234.

17. Poem references are to John Milton, *Paradise Lost*, ed. Gordon Teskey (New York: Norton, 2020).

18. See Martin Luther and Desiderius Erasmus, *Luther and Erasmus: Free Will and Salvation*, ed. E. Gordon Rupp and Phillip S. Watson (Philadelphia: Westminster Press, 1969).

19. John Milton, "An Apology for Smectymnuus," *The Prose Works of John Milton* (London: Westley and Davis, 1835), 81.

20. Milton, "An Apology for Smectymnuus," 81.

21. Milton, "An Apology for Smectymnuus," 81.

22. See the description of Vico's failed attempt for this position in *The Autobiography of Giambattista Vico*, trans. Max Harold Fisch and Thomas Goddard Bergin (Ithaca, N.Y.: Cornell University Press, 1944), 163–64.

23. Vico, *Autobiography of Giambattista Vico*, 200.

24. René Descartes, *Discours sur le méthode*, Gutenberg.org, www.gutenberg.org /files/13846/13846-h/13846-h.htm.

25. See Vico's *De antiquissima Italorum sapientia, ex linguae latinae originibus eruenda* [On the most ancient wisdom of the Italians, unearthed from the origins of the Latin language, 1710], in *Humanistic Education: Six Inaugural Orations, 1699–1707*, trans. Giorgio A. Pinton and Arthur W. Shippee (Ithaca, N.Y.: Cornell University Press, 1944).

26. See Vico, *The New Science of Giambattista Vico* (1744), trans. Thomas Goddard Bergin and Max Harold Fisch (Ithaca, N.Y.: Cornell University Press, 1968).

27. *The New Science of Giambattista Vico*, para. 786.

28. *The New Science of Giambattista Vico*, para. 875.

29. For a study devoted in large part to showing the preeminence of poetic modes of thinking and cultural production in Vico, see Giuseppe Mazzotta, *The New Map of the World: Vico's Poetic Encyclopedia* (Princeton: Princeton University Press, 1999).

30. References to the note are from *Scritti vari e pagine sparse*, ed. Fausto Nicolini, vol. 7 of *Opere* (Bari, Italy: Laterza, 1940), 79–82; trans. in *Dante*, ed. Caesar, 352–55.

31. See *Dante*, ed. Caesar, 354–55.

32. References to the letter are from *L'autobiografia, il carteggio e le poesie varie*, ed. Benedetto Croce and Fausto Nicolini, vol. 5 of *Opere* (Bari, Italy: Laterza, 1929), 195–200; trans. in *Dante*, ed. Caesar 348–52.

33. See *Dante*, ed. Caesar, 349–50.

34. See *Dante*, ed. Caesar, 351–52.

35. Edward Gibbon, *The History of the Decline and Fall of the Roman Empire*, vol. 6, ch. 37, para. 619, Gutenberg.org, www.gutenberg.org/files/25717/25717-h/25717 -h.htm.

36. See my description of the relation between Bettinelli and Voltaire in *Romantic Europe and the Ghost of Italy* (New Haven: Yale University Press, 2008), 110.

37. Bettinelli's protagonist is a now-forgotten poet named Pascali.

38. References are to Saverio Bettinelli, *Lettere virgiliane e inglesi e altri scritti critici*, ed. V. E. Alfieri (Bari, Italy: Laterza, 1930), 9–13; trans. in *Dante*, ed. Caesar, 379–83.

39. John Dryden, "Epistle the Sixth, to the Earl of Roscommon, on His Excellent Essay on Translated Verse" (1684), in vol. 11 of *The Works of John Dryden* (London: William Miller, 1808), 28.

Chapter 5: Romantic Apotheosis

1. See my *Romantic Europe and the Ghost of Italy*, 102.

2. See my *Romantic Europe and the Ghost of Italy*, 98.

3. Thomas Babington Macauley, "Dante and Milton," in Dante Alighieri, *The Divine Comedy*, trans. Henry Wadsworth Longfellow (Leipzig: Bernhard Tauchnitz, 1867), 2:374.

4. See my *Romantic Europe and the Ghost of Italy*, 98.

5. See Renee Winegarten, *Germaine de Staël and Benjamin Constant* (New Haven: Yale University Press, 2008).

6. All references are to Germaine de Staël, *Corinne; or Italy*, trans. Isabel Hill (London: Richard Bentley, 1833), book 2, chapter 3, Gutenberg.org, www.gutenberg.org/files/52077/52077-h/52077-h.htm.

7. See Carlyle's zealous interpretation of *Inferno* 15 as an example of Dante's robust heroism: "It must have been a great solacement to Dante, and was, as we can see, a proud thought for him at times, [that] he, here in exile, could do this work [the *Commedia*]; that no Florence, nor no man or men, could hinder him from doing it, or even much help him in doing it. He knew too, partly, that it was great; the greatest a man could do. 'If thou follow thy star, *Se tu segui la tua stella*,'—so could the Hero [Dante], in his forsakeness, in his extreme need, still say to himself: 'Follow thou thy star, thou shalt not fail of a glorious haven!'" Thomas Carlyle, *On Heroes, Hero-Worship, and the Heroic in History* (London: Chapman and Hall, 1840), 106. In *Inferno* 15, Dante actually questions the preoccupation with worldly glory of his former teacher, Brunetto Latini, who is punished in hell for sodomy. See my discussion of this passage in *Romantic Europe and the Ghost of Italy*, 98–99; and *Botticelli's Secret*, 271n44.

8. See Diego Saglia, "Dante and British Romantic Women Writers: Writing the Nation, Defining National Culture," in *Dante in the Long Nineteenth Century: Nationality, Identity, and Appropriation*, ed. Aida Audeh and Nick Havely (Oxford: Oxford University Press, 2012), 184–203. On Dante's presence among women on the other side of the Atlantic, see Christian Y. Dupont, "'How the Young Women Take to It!' Italian Exiles and Women Readers of Dante in Nineteenth-Century New England," in *Dante Beyond Borders*, ed. Havely et al., 252–64. On the marketing of Dante's to middle-class American matriarchs in the late nineteenth century, see Carol Chiodo, "Dante for Mothers," in *Dante Beyond Borders*, ed. Havely et al., 277–86.

9. On these women authors in relation to how "a female interpretive readership developed under and in reaction to patriarchal influence," see Federica Coluzzi, *Dante Beyond Influence: Rethinking Reception in Victorian Literary Culture* (Manchester: Manchester University Press, 2021), 99.

10. See Saglia, "Dante and British Romantic Women Writers," 196–201.

11. All references are to Mary Shelley, *Frankenstein; or the Modern Prometheus* (1819), Gutenberg.org, www.gutenberg.org/files/84/84-h/84-h.htm#chap24.

12. See, for example, Dante's interpretive exhortation: "O you possessed of sturdy intellects, / observe the teaching that is hidden here / beneath the veil of verses so obscure" (*O voi ch'avete li 'ntelletti sani, / mirate la dottrina che s'asconde / sotto 'l velame de li versi strain, Inf. 9.61–63*).

13. "The greater horn within that ancient flame / began to sway and tremble, murmuring / just like a fire that struggles in the wind" (*Lo maggior corno de la fiamma antica / cominciò a crollarsi mormorando, / pur come quella cui vento affatica, 85–87*).

Chapter 6: Transition and Translation

1. In 2022 alone, several new translations of the *Purgatorio* appeared in English, including ones by Mary Jo Bang and D. M. Black as well as an omnibus volume edited by Nick Havely with Bernard O'Donoghue. See the discussion in Robert Pogue Harrison, "Labors of Love," *New York Review of Books*, December 16, 2021.

2. Toynbee, *Dante in English Literature from Chaucer to Cary (c. 1380–1844)*, 2:80.

3. See my "The Task of Italian Romanticism: Literary Form and Polemic Response," in *The Oxford Handbook of European Romanticism*, ed. Paul Hamilton (Oxford: Oxford University Press, 2016), 377–89.

4. Germaine de Staël, "The Spirit of Translation," trans. Joseph Luzzi, *Romanic Review* 97, no. 3, special issue: *Italy and France: Imagined Geographies* (2006): 279.

5. Madame de Staël, "Spirit of Translation," 279.

6. Madame de Staël, "Spirit of Translation," 280.

7. Diego Saglia, "Translation and Cultural Appropriation: Dante, Paolo and Francesca in British Romanticism," *Quaderns. Revista de traducció* 7 (2002): 106. See Byron, *Letters and Journals*, ed. Leslie A. Marchand, 12 vols. (Cambridge, Mass.: The Belknap Press of Harvard University Press, 1973–82), 3:221.

8. On the enormous influence of Dante's autobiographical epic on Byron, among others, as part of an "aggrandizement of the artist [as] central to what in the nineteenth century came to be called the religion of art," see Paul Barolsky, "Dante and the Modern Cult of the Artist," *Arion* 12, no. 2 (Fall 2004): 2, 6. On Byron's *Don Juan* in terms of Byron's poetic projection of himself as "an image of his self-exile: he sells a mythical, heroic image of himself, but needs Dante's voice to dignify it," see Alex MacMillan, "*L'effetto voluto*: Dantesque Allusion in the Romantic Period," *The Italianist* 25, no. 1 (2005): 23.

9. Byron, *Childe Harold* 4.42.1–2, vol. 2 of *The Complete Poetical Works*, ed. Jerome J. McGann, 7 vols. (Oxford: Clarendon Press, 1980–93).

10. Byron, *Letters and Journals*, 8:40. See Millicent Marcus, "The Italian Body Politic Is a Woman: Feminized National Identity in Postwar Italian Film," in *Sparks and Seeds: Medieval Literature and its Afterlife. Essays in Honour of John Freccero*, ed. Dana E. Stewart and Alison Cornish (Turnhout, Belgium: Brepols, 2000), 329–47.

11. See the discussion in Daryl S. Ogden, "Byron, Italy, and the Poetics of Liberal Imperialism," *Keats-Shelley Journal* 49 (2000): 114–37; and Mauro Pala, "Facets of the Risorgimento: The Debate on the Classical Heritage from Byron's *Childe Harold* to Leopardi's *Canzone ad Angelo Mai*," in *British Romanticism and Italian Literature: Translating, Reviewing, Rewriting*, ed. Laura Bandiera and Diego Saglia (Amsterdam: Rodopi, 2005), 195.

12. On Byron and fellow Romantic authors fashioning Dante into a symbol of liberty and patriotism, see Steve Ellis, *Dante and English Poetry: Shelley to T. S. Eliot* (Cambridge: Cambridge University Press), 20–23.

13. Frederick L Beaty, "Byron and the Story of Francesca da Rimini," *PMLA* 75, no. 4 (1960): 395.

14. Byron, *Letters and Journals*, 8:40. See the discussion in Timothy Webb, "Hunt, Byron, and the Fate of Francesca," in *Dante in the Nineteenth Century: Reception, Canonicity, Popularization*, ed. Nick Havely (New York: Peter Lang, 2011), 44.

15. See Beaty, "Byron and the Story of Francesca da Rimini," 395.

16. Byron, *Letters and Journals*, February 29, 1816, 5:35.

17. See Francesca Buglioni Knox, "*Galeotto fu il libro e chi lo scrisse*: Nineteenth-Century English Translations, Interpretations and Reworkings of Dante's Paolo and Francesca," *Dante Studies* 115 (1997): 223. On the apotheosis of Francesca as Romantic heroine, Francesco De Sanctis holds that Francesca represents both the "finest creation of modern poetry" and "women . . . released from metaphysics"—in short, the poetic ideal of modern womanhood that likely influenced successors including Shakespeare, Goethe, and Byron. De Sanctis, "Francesca da Rimini," 51.

18. See Knox, "*Galeotto fu il libro e chi lo scrisse*," 232. In praising Byron's and Dante Gabriel Rossetti's versions of *Inferno* 5, Knox emphasizes the following four traits: their sensitivity "to the way readers would understand their translations and to the cultural context of Dante's original"; their combined knowledge of Italian and mastery of English poetic composition; their ability to "reproduce what they believed were Dante's ambiguities rather than impose their own interpretations"; and how both authors "stamped their translations with their own poetic sensibility" (233–34).

19. Byron's use of *terza rima* drew on his long-standing defense of this metrical form, expressed in the form of a meditation on Miltonic blank verse: "I am not persuaded that the Paradise Lost would not have been more nobly conveyed to posterity, not perhaps in heroic couplets, although even *they* could sustain the subject if

well balanced, but in the stanza of Spenser or of Tasso, or in the terza rima of Dante, which the powers of Milton could easily have grafted on our language." Byron, *Letters and Journals of Lord Byron, with Notices of His Life*, ed. Thomas Moore, 6 vols. (London: John Murray, 1854), 5:20. Javier Ortiz-García connects Byron's use of *terza rima* in the Paolo and Francesca episode to his larger theory and practice of translation. Ortiz-García, "Lord Byron y la traducción," *Hermēneus. Revista de Traducción e Interpretación* 10 (2008): 8–9.

20. See Saglia, "Translation and Cultural Appropriation," 116. "Apparently an exercise in linguistic accuracy, his text is also entangled in the larger Romantic discourse of the liberal Dante and may thus be taken as a (temporary) point of arrival of a progress through Romantic translation as appropriation, and its links with rewriting, politics and literary criticism."

21. Wordsworth's politically inflected reading of Dante is the subject of my "Wordsworth, Dante, and British Romantic Identity," in *Romantic Europe and the Ghost of Italy*, 141–59.

22. Byron, *The Confessions of Lord Byron: A Collection of His Private Opinions of Men and of Matters*, ed. W. A. Lewis Bettany (London: John Murray, 1905), 242.

23. See John Freccero, "The Portrait of Francesca: *Inferno* 5," in *In Dante's Wake: Reading from Medieval to Modern in the Augustinian Tradition*, ed. Danielle Callegari and Melissa Swain (New York: Fordham University Press, 2015), ss19.

24. Nick Havely, "Francesca Frustrated: New Evidence About Hobhouse's and Byron's Translation of Pellico's *Francesca da Rimini*," *Romanticism* 1 (1995): 107.

25. All references to Longfellow's poetry are to *The Complete Poetical Works of Henry Wadsworth Longfellow* (Boston: Houghton Mifflin, 1902), Gutenberg.org, www.gutenberg.org/ebooks/1365.

26. See Milton's Sonnet 19 and its Dantesque gesture to the midway point in life ("Ere half my days"):

> When I consider how my light is spent
> Ere half my days, in this dark world and wide,
> And that one talent which is death to hide
> Lodged with me useless . . .

In a similarly Dantesque vein, Milton's preoccupation with fulfilling his potential and his own sense of mission was a long-standing one, going back to his youthful poem "On His Having Arrived at the Age of Twenty-Three" and its talk of a poetic development as of yet devoid of "bud or blossom":

> How soon hath Time, the subtle thief of youth,
> Stolen on his wing my three-and-twentieth year!
> My hasting days fly on with full career,
> But my late spring no bud or blossom sheweth.

John Milton, *The Complete English Poems*, ed. Gordon Campbell (New York: Everyman's Library, 1992), 96, 166.

27. On Longfellow's relation to Dante, see *Dante Studies* 128 (2010), special volume: *Longfellow and Dante*, ed. Giuseppe Mazzotta and Arielle Saiber.

28. See Kathleen Verduin, "Dante in the Life of Longfellow," *Dante Studies* 128 (2010): 17.

29. See Verduin, "Dante in the Life of Longfellow," 17.

30. See Verduin, "Dante in the Life of Longfellow," 17.

31. For a description of Fanny Longfellow's accidental death, see Nicholas A. Basbanes, *A Life of Henry Wadsworth Longfellow* (New York: Knopf, 2020), 320–31.

32. Basbanes, *A Life of Henry Wadsworth Longfellow*, 322, 329.

33. Henry Wadsworth Longfellow, letter to Mary Appleton Mackintosh, *The Letters of Henry Wadsworth Longfellow*, ed. Andrew Hilen (Cambridge, Mass.: Harvard University Press, 1972).

34. See Sigmund Freud, "Mourning and Melancholia," in *The Standard Edition of the Complete Psychological Works of Sigmund Freud*, ed. James Strachey (London: Hogarth Press, 1953–74), 14:243–58.

35. Theodore Wesley Koch, *Dante in America: A Historical and Bibliographical Study* (Boston: Ginn, 1896), 40.

36. See Longfellow, *Letters*; and Koch, *Dante in America*, 40.

37. For a fictional representation of these Dantesque encounters, see Matthew Pearl, *The Dante Club* (New York: Random House, 2003).

38. See Longfellow, *Letters*; and Koch, *Dante in America*, 42.

39. These remarks draw on my essay "How to Read Dante in the Twenty-First Century," *The American Scholar*, March 22, 2016, https://theamericanscholar.org /how-to-read-dante-in-the-21st-century/.

40. See, for example, Byron's *The Prophecy of Dante* (1821) as well as Shelley's "Ode to the West Wind" (1819) and *The Triumph of Life* (1822).

41. See my "How to Read Dante in the Twenty-First Century."

42. See my "How to Read Dante in the Twenty-First Century."

43. On the detractors of Longfellow's adherence to a literal translation of Dante, see Angelina La Piana, *Dante's American Pilgrimage: A Historical Survey of Dante Studies in the United States, 1800–1944* (New Haven: Yale University Press, 1948), 100–102.

44. Walter Benjamin discusses how the "task of the translator consists in finding that intended effect [*Intention*] upon the language into which he is translating which produces in it the echo of the original," which is a fitting gloss on the intensely dialogic link between English and Tuscan in Longfellow's translation of the *Commedia*.

NOTES TO CHAPTER 7 205

Benjamin, "The Task of the Translator," in *Illuminations*, trans. Harry Zohn (New York: Schocken, 1969), 70.

45. La Piana, *Dante's American Pilgrimage*, 109–10.

Chapter 7: The Modernist Dante

1. The literature on Dante's influence on T. S. Eliot is vast. See Audrey T. Rodgers, "T. S. Eliot's 'Purgatorio': The Structure of *Ash-Wednesday*," *Comparative Literature* 7, no. 1 (March 1970): 112n1, for a catalogue of some of the key voices on Dante's influence on Eliot's poetry, including Nunzio Cossu, "Dantismo Politicoreligioso di T. S. Eliot," *Nuova antologia* 495 (1965): 181–91; and Mario Praz, "Thomas Stearns Eliot," *Terzo programma* 2 (1965): 87–163. More recently, see Ellis, *Dante and English Poetry*, 210–43; and Dominic Manganiello, *T. S. Eliot and Dante* (Basingstoke, England: Macmillan Press, 1989). For a selection of Eliot's writings on Dante, see *Dante in English*, ed. Eric Griffiths and Matthew Reynolds (London: Penguin, 2005), 311–20.

2. T. S. Eliot, "A Talk on Dante," *Kenyon Review* 14 (Spring 1952): 178.

3. T. S. Eliot, "Dante," in *Selected Essays*, ed. Frank Kermode (London: Faber and Faber, 1972), 251.

4. Eliot, "A Talk on Dante," 187–88.

5. References to "Prufrock" are from Eliot's *Poems* (New York: Alfred A. Knopf, 1920), Gutenberg.org, www.gutenberg.org/ebooks/1567.

6. I am indebted to Robert Pogue Harrison's "Comedy and Modernity in Dante's Hell," for its general juxtaposition of Ulysses' speech with Guido's and its points on how "the tragic grandeur of Ulysses gives way in the next canto to the small contemporary stature of Guido da Montefeltro." Harrison, "Comedy and Modernity in Dante's Hell," *MLN: Italian* 105, no. 5 (December 1987): 1048.

7. Carlyle, *On Heroes, Hero-Worship, and the Heroic in History*, 106.

8. T. S. Eliot, "Tradition and the Individual Talent" (1919), in *The Sacred Wood: Essays on Poetry and Criticism* (London: Methuen, 1948), 52–53.

9. See, respectively, Keats's letters to his brothers George and Thomas (December 21, 1817) and to Richard Woodhouse (October 27, 1818), in *The Letters of John Keats*, ed. Hyder E. Rollins (Cambridge, Mass.: Harvard University Press, 1958).

10. Eliot, "Tradition and the Individual Talent," 56.

11. See Douglas Bush, "T. S. Eliot," in *Engaged and Disengaged* (Cambridge, Mass.: Harvard University Press, 1966), 98.

12. T. S. Eliot, *Four Quartets* (London: Faber and Faber, 1959).

13. T. S. Eliot, "What Dante Means to Me," *To Criticize the Critic and Other Writings* (London: Faber and Faber, 1965), 125. See the discussion in Eloise Hay,

"T. S. Eliot's Virgil: Dante," *Journal of English and Germanic Philology* 82, no. 1 (January 1983): 50–51.

14. For a broad consideration of Dante's impact on Modernism, see Ricardo J. Quinones, "Dante and Modernism," *Annali d'Italianistica* 8 (1990): 30–36.

15. Stuart Hirschberg, "A Dialogue Between Realism and Idealism in Yeats's 'Ego Dominus Tuus,'" *Colby Quarterly* 11, no. 2 (June 1975): 129–30.

16. References to the poem are from William Butler Yeats, *The Collected Poems of W. B. Yeats*, ed. Richard Finneran (New York: Scribner, 1996), 160–61.

17. For a study of Yeats's complex understanding of the Romantic elements in Dante, see George Bornstein, "Yeats's Romantic Dante," *Colby Quarterly* 15, no. 2 (June 1979): 93–113.

18. W. H. Auden, "Yeats: Master of Diction," *Saturday Review of Literature*, June 8, 1940, in *The Complete Works of W. H. Auden, Volume II, 1939–1948: Prose*, ed. Edward Mendelsohn (Princeton: Princeton University Press, 1993), 63.

19. For Guido Cavalcanti's lyrical takedown of Dante, see his Sonnet 23, "To Dante, rebuking him for his way of life after the death of Beatrice," in David Anderson, *Pound's Cavalcanti: An Edition of the Translations, Notes, and Essays* (Princeton: Princeton University Press, 1983), 91. On Pound's relation to Dante, see Matthew T. Reynolds, "Ezra Pound: Quotations and Continuity," in *Dante's Modern Afterlife: Reception and Response from Blake to Heaney*, ed. Nick Havely (New York: St. Martin's Press, 1997), 113–27.

20. Bornstein, "Yeats's Romantic Dante," 109.

21. Ernest Hemingway, *A Moveable Feast* (New York: Touchstone, 1992), 110.

22. Ezra Pound, "From *Dante*," in *The Poet's Dante*, ed. Hawkins and Jacoff, 6.

23. See Ezra Pound, "A Retrospect," in *Literary Essays of Ezra Pound*, ed. T. S. Eliot (London: Faber and Faber, 1954), 10; and the discussion in Stephen Paul Ellis, "Dante in Pound's Early Career," *Paideuma: Modern and Contemporary Poetry and Poetics* 8, no. 3 (Winter 1979): 552.

24. Pound, *Spirit of Romance*, 167. See the discussion in Ellis, "Dante in Pound's Early Career," 553.

25. Eliot, "A Talk on Dante," 181.

26. Richard Ellmann, *James Joyce* (Oxford: Oxford University Press, 1959), 2.

27. See Ellmann, *James Joyce*, 226. The literature on Joyce's relation to Dante is vast; I will single out Howard Helsinger, "Joyce and Dante," *ELH* 35, no. 4 (December 1968): 591–605; Mary Trackett Reynolds, *Joyce and Dante: The Shaping Imagination* (Princeton: Princeton University Press, 1981); Lucia Boldrini, *Joyce, Dante, and the Poetics of Literary Relations: Language and Meaning in "Finnegans Wake"* (Cambridge: Cambridge University Press, 2001); and James Robinson, *Joyce's Dante: Exile, Memory, and Community* (Cambridge: Cambridge University Press, 2006).

28. James Joyce, *A Portrait of the Artist as a Young Man* (London: Penguin, 1993), 275.

29. Helsinger, "Joyce and Dante," 592; Robinson, *Joyce's Dante*, 78.

30. Piero Boitani, "Irish Dante: Yeats, Joyce, Beckett," in *Metamorphosing Dante: Appropriations, Manipulations, and Rewritings in the Twentieth and Twenty-First Centuries*, ed. Manuele Gragnolati, Fabio Camilletti, and Fabian Lampart (Vienna: Turia + Kant, 2010), 44.

31. Boitani, "Irish Dante," 44. See also his reading of the parallels between Dante's and Joyce's versions of Ulysses (44–48).

32. Cited in Reynolds, *Joyce and Dante*, 208.

33. The opening line of Joyce's *Finnegans Wake* playfully references Vico, who like Joyce was celebrated for his fascination with the history of words and their etymological inflections: "riverrun, past Eve and Adam's, from swerve of shore to bend of bay, brings us by a commodious *vicus* of recirculation back to Howth Castle and Environs" *Finnegans Wake* (London: Penguin, 2000), 1, emphasis added. On Joyce's relation to Vico, see Donald Verene, ed., *Vico and Joyce* (New York: SUNY Press, 1987).

34. See the Gabler edition of James Joyce, *Ulysses* (New York: Vintage, 1986), 31.

35. Joyce, *Ulysses*, 644.

36. Joyce, *A Portrait of the Artist as a Young Man*, 276.

Chapter 8: On Heroes and Hero-Worship

1. The title of this chapter echoes the text where the "heroic Dante" is most explicitly developed: Carlyle's *On Heroes, Hero-Worship, and the Heroic in History* (1840); see chapter 5, note 7 above.

2. Primo Levi, *If This Is a Man*, vol. 1 of *The Complete Works of Primo Levi*, ed. Ann Goldstein, 3 vols. (New York: Liveright, 2015), 105.

3. Levi, *If This Is a Man*, 108. The edition uses Mandelbaum's translation of Dante.

4. Levi, *If This Is a Man*, 108. Dante's original reads: "Considerate la vostra semenza: / fatti non foste a viver come bruti / ma per seguir virtute e canoscenza" (*Inf.* 26.118–20). See chapter 5 for my discussion of how this same speech from Ulysses resurfaced in Mary Shelley's *Frankenstein* when Victor Frankenstein exhorted the stranded sailors to pursue his monster at great peril to all.

5. Levi, *If This Is a Man*, 108.

6. Levi, *If This Is a Man*, 108.

7. Levi, *If This Is a Man*, 109. Dante's original reads: "infin che 'l mar fu sovra noi rinchiuso" (*Inf.* 26.142).

8. Osip Mandelstam, "The Stalin Epigram," in *Selected Poems*, trans. Clarence Brown and W. S. Merwin (New York: Atheneum, 1974), no. 286, p. 70.

9. Osip Mandelstam, "Conversation About Dante," trans. Jane Gary Harris and Constance Link, in *The Poet's Dante*, ed. Hawkins and Jacoff, 40–93.

10. Mandelstam, "Conversation About Dante," 40–41.

11. See Wai Chee Dimock, "Literature for the Planet," *PMLA* 116, no. 1 (January 2001): 179–80; and Seamus Heaney, "The Government of the Tongue," in *The Government of the Tongue: Selected Prose, 1978–1987* (New York: Noonday, 1988), 98.

12. Mandelstam, "Conversation About Dante," 43.

13. Not coincidentally, the British author Julian Barnes titled his novel from 2016 about Shostakovich, who shared some of Mandelstam's bitter experiences in the Stalinist Soviet Union, *The Noise of Time*.

14. Mandelstam, "Conversation About Dante," 49.

15. Mandelstam, "Conversation About Dante," 67.

16. Mandelstam, "Conversation About Dante," 90.

17. Quintin Hoare and Geoffrey Nowell Smith, introduction to Antonio Gramsci, *Selections from the Prison Notebooks*, eds. Quintin Hoare and Geoffrey Nowell Smith (New York: International Publishers, 1971), lxxxix.

18. Hoare and Smith, *Selections from the Prison Notebooks*, xcii.

19. Antonio Gramsci, "Il cieco Tiresia," *Sotto la mole, 1916–1920* (Turin: Einaudi, 1960), 392–93. See also the discussion in Frank Rosengarten, "Gramsci's 'Little Discovery': Gramsci's Interpretation of Canto X of Dante's *Inferno*," *boundary 2* 14, no. 3, special issue: *The Legacy of Antonio Gramsci* (Spring 1986): 76.

20. Antonio Gramsci, *Prison Notebooks*, ed. and trans. Joseph Buttigeig, 3 vols. (New York: Columbia University Press, 1992), 2:247.

21. Gramsci, *Prison Notebooks*, 2:247.

22. "a te fia bello / averti fatta parte per te stesso," "your honor will / be best kept if your party is your self" (*Par.* 17.68–69).

Chapter 9: Dante on Screen

1. See Barolini, Commento Baroliniano, https://digitaldante.columbia.edu/dante/divine-comedy/inferno/inferno-5/.

2. Peter Bondanella and Federico Pacchioni, *A History of Italian Cinema* (New York: Bloomsbury, 2017), 7.

3. Bondanella and Pacchioni, *A History of Italian Cinema*, 6.

4. See John P. Welle, "Early Cinema, Dante's *Inferno*, and the Origins of Italian Film Culture," in *Dante, Cinema, and Television*, ed. Amilcare Iannucci (Toronto: University of Toronto Press, 2004), 22.

5. See Amilcare Ianucci, "Dante and Hollywood," in *Dante, Cinema and Television*, ed. Iannucci, 10.

6. See Ianucci, "Dante and Hollywood," 11.

7. For a discussion of Scorsese as a "contemporary Dante" and a list of the Dantesque allusions and themes in his works, see Catherine O'Brien, *Martin Scorsese's Divine Comedy: Movies and Religion* (New York: Bloomsbury, 2018), 4–8.

8. On Dante's palinodic tendency and its relation to the construction of his authorial self, see Albert Russell Ascoli, *Dante and the Making of the Modern Author* (Cambridge: Cambridge University Press, 2008).

9. For the paradigmatic articulation of the auteur's vision of the camera as "pen," see Alexandre Astruc, "The Birth of a New Avant-Garde: *La Caméra-Stylo*," in *The New Wave*, ed. Peter Graham (London: Martin Secker and Warburg Limited, 1968), 17–23. On auteur cinema and its "essayistic" qualities, see Timothy B. Corrigan, *The Essay Film: From Montaigne, After Marker* (Oxford: Oxford University Press, 2011).

10. On the Dantesque elements of *La dolce vita*, see Bondanella and Pacchioni, *A History of Italian Cinema*, who call Fellini's film "a modern-day *Divine Comedy*" (252); see also Barbara K. Lewalski, "Federico Fellini's 'Purgatorio,'" *Massachusetts Review* 5, no. 3 (Spring 1964): 567–73, which describes Marcello's friend Steiner as an "anti-Virgil" and also considers Fellini's debt to Dante in his deeply interior *8½*. On the Dantesque elements of *La dolce vita*, see also P. Adams Sitney, *Vital Crises in Italian Cinema: Iconography, Stylistics, Politics* (Oxford: Oxford University Press, 2015), 109–16.

11. Pier Paolo Pasolini, "The 'Cinema of Poetry,'" in *Heretical Empiricism*, trans. Ben Lawton and Louise Barnett (Bloomington: Indiana University Press, 1988), 167–86; Sitney, *Vital Crises in Italian Cinema*, 202–3.

12. On the ironies inherent in Godard's choice of Cinecittà as the film's setting and his allusions to the "death of film" vis-à-vis Hollywood, see Jacques Aumont, "The Fall of the Gods: Jean-Luc Godard's *Le Mépris* (1963)," in *French Film: Texts and Contexts*, ed. Susan Hayward and Ginette Vincendau (London: Routledge, 2006), 175.

13. See Brian Udoff, "Kieślowski: Cinema's Dante?," *The Johns Hopkins Newsletter*, November 4, 2010: "The trilogy could be the equivalent of *The Divine Comedy* in the way the structure is so carefully woven into the tales to create a film playful yet dense, and immediately recognizable as art without alienating the average viewer."

14. David Trumbore, "Hollywood! Adapt This: Dante Alighieri's *The Divine Comedy*," *Collider*, September 22, 2013, https://collider.com/dante-alighieri-the-divine-comedy-movie-adaptation/.

15. Matthew Razak, "WB Scoops up Dante's *Inferno* Film," *Flixist*, February 20, 2020, www.flixist.com/wb-scoops-up-dante-s-inferno-film/.

16. For example, Bruno Acosta, a contemporary filmmaker, has created documentaries and animated pieces on the *Commedia*. For information on his *Dante's Hell Animated* (2013), see IMDB, www.imdb.com/title/tt1472122/.

Chapter 10: Trigger Warnings and Papal Blessings

1. Nick Squires, "Dante's Divine Comedy 'Offensive and Should Be Banned,'" *The Telegraph*, March 13, 2012, www.telegraph.co.uk/culture/culturenews/9140869 /Dantes-Divine-Comedy-offensive-and-should-be-banned.html.

2. Squires, "Dante's Divine Comedy 'Offensive and Should Be Banned.'"

3. Gherush 92, "Via *La Divina Commedia* dalle scuole," www.gherush92.com /news.asp?tipo=A&id=2985.

4. For a discussion of the proposed ban by Gherush 92 in the context of how Dante is taught today, see Kristina Olson, "Ideology and Pedagogy: The Tensions of Teaching," *Dante Studies* 137 (2019): 124–26. In this same volume, the Gherush 92 controversy is examined in relation to such issues as teaching Dante amid current debates about sexuality and race (Gary Cestaro, "Dante Spinning Forward," 127–37); calls to erase Dante from Italian school curricula (Claudio Giunta, "Perché continuiamo a leggere la *Commedia*?," 151–70); discomfort in the classroom and Dante's own poetics of "defamation" (Franziska Meier, "Defaming Dante," 187–96); multicultural tendencies in Dante (Akash Kumar, "Appreciating the Whole: Dante Now," 178–86); the poet's reticence toward the cultural plurality discussed in the previous entry (Vittorio Montemaggi, "Love, Ideology, and Inter-Religious Relations in the *Commedia*," 197–209); and the teaching of religion today (Peter S. Hawkins, "Divinity School Dante," 171–77).

5. Squires, "Dante's Divine Comedy 'Offensive and Should Be Banned.'"

6. Thu-Huong Ha, "Texas Bans 15,000 Books from State Prisons, Including Dante's 'Inferno' and 'The Color Purple,'" *Route Fifty*, July 5, 2017, www.route-fifty .com/management/2016/09/texas-bans-15000-books-state-prisons-including -dantes-inferno-and-color-purple/131886/.

7. Nahib Bulos, "No 'Divine Comedy,' no 'One Hundred Years of Solitude': Book Banning in Kuwait Draws the Ire of the Intellectual Class," *Los Angeles Times*, October 1, 2018, www.latimes.com/world/la-fg-kuwait-book-ban-20181001-story.html.

8. See Catherine Keen, "Dante's *Fortuna*: An Overview of Canon Formation and National Contexts," in *Ethics, Politics, and Justice in Dante*, ed. Giulia Gaimari and Catherine Keen (London: University College London, 2019), 129–43.

9. "The Dante Celebration at Florence: Letter from Victor Hugo," *New York Times*, June 5, 1885, www.nytimes.com/1865/06/05/archives/the-dante-celebration -at-florence-letter-from-victor-hugo.html.

10. Visual proof of Fascist appropriation of literary figures and their transformation into warrior-like figures may be found in the monument to Petrarch in Arezzo, initially designed by Alessandro Lazzerini in 1907 and brought to completion in 1928 under Mussolini; and the statue of Ugo Foscolo by Antonio Berti in Florence's

Cathedral of Santa Croce from 1935–37, which I discuss in *Romantic Europe and the Ghost of Italy*, 163–65.

11. For studies of this project, see Thomas L. Schumacher, *The Danteum* (New York: Princeton Architectural Press, 1985); and Aarati Kanekar, "From Building to Poem and Back: The Danteum as a Study in the Projection of Meaning Across Symbolic Forms," *Journal of Architecture* 10 (April 2005): 135–59.

12. Matteo Pucciarelli, "Sangiuliano: 'Dante è il fondatore del pensiero di destra italiano.' Un caso le parole del ministro della Cultura," *La Repubblica*, January 14, 2023, www.repubblica.it/politica/2023/01/14/news/sangiuliano_dante_destra -383535459/.

13. See "*Inferno* by Dante Alighieri," *Book Trigger Warnings*, https://booktriggerwarnings.com/index.php?title=Inferno_by_Dante_Alighieri.

14. As Nick Havely wryly—and rightly—observed about Dante's being promoted as a defender of Britain's role in the European Union, "I expect it would be quite a dangerous thing to try to recruit Dante to your cause, whether left-wing or right-wing." Thea Lenarduzzi, "The Best Books on Dante, Recommended by Nick Havely," *Five Books*, October 5, 2017, https://fivebooks.com/best-books/dante-nick -havely/.

15. Ian Thomson, "*The Divine Comedy*: The Greatest Single Work of Western Literature," *Irish Times*, September 8, 2018, www.irishtimes.com/culture/books/the -divine-comedy-the-greatest-single-work-of-western-literature-1.3619042. For a discussion of Benigni's wildly successful live performance *TuttoDante*, a monologue about *The Divine Comedy*, see Ben Sisario, "Funnyman Takes on Dante's 'Comedy,'" *New York Times*, May 22, 2009, www.nytimes.com/2009/05/23/theater/23dant. html.

16. Pope Benedict XV's references to Dante are from his "In Praeclara Summorum," www.vatican.va/content/benedict-xv/en/encyclicals/documents/hf_ben-xv _enc_30041921_in-praeclara-summorum.html.

17. Pope Paul VI's references to Dante are from his "Altissimi Cantus," December 7, 1965, https://d2y1pz2y630308.cloudfront.net/2287/documents/2016/12 /PPaulVIMotuPro2.htm. When necessary, I modify papal citation of Dante's original *Commedia* to its correct form.

18. Pope Francis's references to Dante are from his apostolic letter, "Candor Lucis Aeternae," March 25, 2021, www.vatican.va/content/francesco/en/apost_letters /documents/papa-francesco-lettera-ap_20210325_centenario-dante.html. The English translations in Francis's letter are from Henry Wadsowrth Longfellow's translation of *The Divine Comedy* (Boston: Ticknor and Fields, 1867).

19. See especially Francis's lengthy citation of Paul VI's words: "Paul VI went on to illustrate what makes the *Comedy* a source of spiritual enrichment accessible to

everyone. 'Dante's poem is universal: in its immense scope, it embraces heaven and earth, eternity and time, divine mysteries and human events, sacred doctrine and teachings drawn from the light of reason, the fruits of personal experience and the annals of history.'" "Candor Lucis Aeternae."

20. Peter S. Hawkins, "Poema Sacro," *Annali d'Italianistica* 25: *Literature, Religion, and the Sacred* (2007): 199.

21. For a recent study of how the *Commedia* can be productively read from our modern perspective and in full awareness of the distance between today's sensibilities and those informing Dante's own medieval context, see Alison Cornish, *Believing in Dante: Truth in Fiction* (Cambridge: Cambridge University Press, 2022).

Index

Page numbers followed by an f or t refer to figures or the timeline.